Special Issue
Development, Evaluation, and Treatment of Students with Behavior Disorders
Guest Editors:
Melissa A. Bray and Melissa Stormont

AIMS AND SCOPE

Psychology in the Schools is a bimonthly peer-reviewed journal devoted to research, opinion, and practice. The journal welcomes theoretical and applied manuscripts, focusing on the issues confronting school psychologists, teachers, counselors, administrators, and other personnel workers in schools and colleges, public and private organizations. Preferences will be given to manuscripts that clearly describe implications for the practitioner in the schools.

Psychology in the Schools (Print ISSN: 0033-3085; Online ISSN: 1520-6807 at Wiley Interscience, www.interscience.wiley.com) is published bimonthly in January, March, May, July, September, and November by Wiley Subscription Services, Inc., a Wiley Company, 605 Third Avenue, New York, NY 10158. Periodicals postage paid at New York, NY and at additional mailing offices.

Subscription price (Volume 39, 2002): Print only: $325.00 in U.S., $367.00 In Canada, Mexico, and outside North America. Electronic only: $325.00 worldwide. A combination price of $342.00 in US., $384.00 in Canada, Mexico, and outside North America, includes the subscription in both electronic and print formats. All subscriptions containing a print element, shipped outside U.S., will be sent by air. Payment must be made in U.S. dollars drawn on U.S. bank. Claims for undelivered copies will be accepted only after the following issue has been delivered. Please enclose a copy of the mailing label. Missing copies will be supplied when losses have been sustained in transit and where reserve stock permits. Please allow four weeks for processing a change of address. For subscription inquiries, please call 212-850-6645; e-mail: subinfo@wiley.com

Postmaster: Send address changes to *Psychology in the Schools*, Caroline Rothaug, Director, Subscription Fulfillment and Sales, Subscription Department, c/o John Wiley & Sons, Inc., 605 Third Ave., New York, NY 10158.

Advertising Sales: Inquiries concerning advertising should be forwarded to Advertising Sales Manager, c/o John Wiley & Sons, Inc., 605 Third Ave., New York, NY 10158; 212-850-8832. Advertising Sales, European Contact: Jackie Sibley, John Wiley & Sons, Ltd., Baffins Lane, Chichester, West Sussex, P019 1UD, England. Tel: 44(0) 1243 770 351; Fax: 44(0) 1243 770 432; e-mail: adsales@wiley.co.uk.

Reprints: Reprint sales and inquiries should be directed to the Customer Service Dept., c/o John Wiley & Sons, Inc., 605 Third Ave., New York, NY 10158. Tel: 212-850-8789. Fax: 212-850-6021.

Manuscripts (four copies) should be submitted to LeAdelle Phelps, Editor, *Psychology in the Schools*, 409 Baldy Hall, Department of Counseling and Educational Psychology, State University of New York at Buffalo, Buffalo, New York 14260. E-mail: Phelps@acsu.buffalo.edu

Other Correspondence should be addressed to *Psychology in the Schools*, Publisher, Professional/Trade Group, c/o John Wiley & Sons, Inc., 605 Third Ave., New York, NY 10158.

Indexing and Abstracting: The contents of this journal are indexed or abstracted in: *Psychological Abstracts; Exceptional Child Education Resources; Child Development Abstracts; The Psychological Readers' Guide; Current Contents; Social and Behavioral Sciences; Current Index to Journals in Education; Education Index; Exceptional Child Education Abstracts; Educational Administration Abstracts; Chicorel Abstracts to Reading and Learning Disabilities; Special Educational Needs Abstracts; and Multicultural Education Abstracts.*

Editorial Production, Wiley Periodicals, Inc.: Paul Dlugokencky

⊗ **This paper meets the requirements of ANSIINISO Z39.48-1992 (Permanence of Paper).**

Volume XXXIX   March 2002   Number 2

Special Issue:
Development, Evaluation, and Treatment
of Students with Behavior Disorders
Guest Editors:
Melissa A. Bray and Melissa Stormont

This Journal is Online.
WILEY
InterScience®
www.interscience.wiley.com

Volume 39, Number 2 was mailed the week of February 18, 2002.

Psychology in the Schools, Vol. 39(2), 2002
© 2002 Wiley Periodicals, Inc.   DOI: 10.1002/pits.10024

FOREWORD TO THE SPECIAL ISSUE: DEVELOPMENT, EVALUATION, AND TREATMENT OF STUDENTS WITH BEHAVIOR DISORDERS

MELISSA A. BRAY

University of Connecticut

MELISSA STORMONT

University of Missouri

Perhaps one of the most arduous and time-consuming tasks faced by classroom teachers and parents is the promotion of appropriate behavior in children with behavior disorders. To support appropriate behavior across multiple settings, professionals need to have access to effective assessment and intervention strategies. In addition, there must be an understanding of school and family characteristics that may be contributing to or sustaining problematic student behavior. Accordingly, this special issue presents a series of articles that focus on the development, assessment, and treatment of children that exhibit disruptive behavior in classrooms, at play, and home.

Melissa Stormont's article on the development of externalizing disorders in preschool children reviews the correlates and contributing factors to the development of externalizing behavior in young children. Child, family, and teacher characteristics that may support problem behavior are the focus of the first part of this article. The second part reviews screening and intervention strategies that could be used within the school setting to help identify children who are at risk for sustaining externalizing problems. In addition, class-wide and individual strategies to promote appropriate behavior are discussed.

In concert with recent federal mandates, Daniel Olympia and his colleagues at the University of Utah, describe functional behavior assessment within the context of methodologies that promote the design of interventions. Their survey of multifaceted functional assessment strategies includes an orientation to efficient technology- and computer-based data collection techniques.

A review of the efficacy of daily behavior report cards is presented by Sandra Chafouleas, T. Chris Riley-Tillman, and James McDougal. They note that daily report cards, employed as both a monitoring and intervention technique, are both effective in increasing appropriate student behavior and parent/teacher communication. However, due to a dearth of empirically based research support, they suggest caution in the widespread acceptance of the technique.

Phillip Belfiore from Mercyhurst College and David Lee and Danielle Klein from Pennsylvania State University provide a new model for researchers to use in classroom-managed research. This new model, applies behavioral action research, and provides a framework that includes variables from applied behavior and action research. They further illustrate how researchers can use the new model by applying the key principles within a classroom-based intervention.

Timothy Lewis, Lisa Powers, Michele Kelk, and Lori Newcomer from the University of Missouri investigate the effectiveness of school-wide positive behavior supports on reducing problem behavior on the playground. They illuminate the importance of providing empirical data on the use of positive behavior support as a preventative strategy for challenging behavior. The study specifically examines the use of both directly teaching appropriate playground behavior and using a group contingency to reduce the frequency of problem behavior on the playground.

Christopher Skinner and his colleagues review the empirical support for reducing social interaction problems by encouraging students to report incidents of prosocial behaviors observed in their classmates. They stipulate that the use of these techniques is appropriate because they do not adversely affect students' social relationships compared to management systems that incorporate student tattling and punishment.

Thomas Kehle and his colleagues review the research on self-modeling as an intervention to decrease disruptive classroom behavior in students with serious emotional disturbance. They suggest that when these students view a change in their behavior, as shown on edited self-modeling intervention videotapes, their memories and self-beliefs subsequently change to be in accord with that depicted on the edited videotape.

Amy Assemany at the University at Albany and David McIntosh at Ball State State University address the negative treatment outcomes of parent training programs for students exhibiting disruptive behaviors and their parents. They review the literature that has clearly demonstrated several environmental stressors associated with dysfunctional families and discuss their relationship to negative treatment outcomes. They conclude with suggestions for future research in this area.

In conclusion, these articles address a diverse representation of assessment and intervention strategies for use with children with behavior disorders. Further, this special issue clearly illuminates the scope of current research agendas in this area. Given the unique needs of students with behavior disorders and the complex and often negative interactions that they engage in with others, multiple areas of research are required to investigate the efficacy of specific assessment and intervention strategies. Overall, the need is clear for future research in all areas addressed in this special issue.

Psychology in the Schools, Vol. 39(2), 2002
© 2002 Wiley Periodicals, Inc.

DOI: 10.1002/pits.10025

EXTERNALIZING BEHAVIOR PROBLEMS IN YOUNG CHILDREN: CONTRIBUTING FACTORS AND EARLY INTERVENTION

MELISSA STORMONT

University of Missouri–Columbia

Early intervention should begin as soon as relatively stable problem behavior is detected in young children. Once professionals have identified young children who are at risk for stable externalizing behavior problems, it is important that they use and/or recommend research-based interventions. Therefore, the first purpose of this article is to present research on specific child (e.g., temperament), family (e.g., family adversity), and transactional characteristics that have been documented to contribute to the manifestation of externalizing disorders in young children. School factors that may also support externalizing behavior in young children will also be presented and include negative teacher interactions and limited support for appropriate behavior. The second purpose of this manuscript is to present screening and intervention strategies that school psychologists could may use with young children who have externalizing behavior prior to or as soon as they enter the kindergarten setting. © 2002 Wiley Periodicals, Inc.

It is important to identify young children at great risk for future behavior problems in order to initiate systematic and early interventions (Walker, 1998). Earliest possible intervention is important for these children due to their increased risk of maintaining and perhaps developing more severe behavior problems (Webster-Stratton, 1997). Research has documented that parent ratings of preschool children's behavior problems were the strongest predictor of antisocial behavior disorders at a 6-year follow-forward assessment (White, Moffitt, Earls, Robins, & Silva, 1990). Other research has similarly documented that preschool and kindergarten children with externalizing behavior were at risk for having future behavior problems and difficulty with peer relationships (Egeland, Kalkoske, Gottesman, & Erickson, 1990; Vitaro, Tremblay, Gagnon, & Biovin, 1992; Vitaro, Tremblay, Gagnon, & Pelletier, 1994). Furthermore, in a review of the research in this area, Webster-Stratton has concluded that "the primary developmental pathway for serious conduct disorders in adolescence and adulthood appears to be established in the preschool period" (p. 432).

To this end it is important that professionals understand the characteristics of young children who are at risk for severe and stable externalizing behavior problems. It is also critical that professionals are aware of methods for screening young children for externalizing problems. In addition, once professionals have identified young children who are at risk for stable externalizing problems, it is important that they use and/or recommend research-based interventions.

Therefore, the first purpose of this manuscript is to briefly present research on specific child (e.g., temperament), family (e.g., family adversity), and parent–child interaction characteristics that have been documented to contribute to the manifestation of externalizing disorders in young children. For more thorough reviews of this information, see Kaiser and Hester (1997), Webster-Stratton (1997), and Campbell (1998). In addition, school factors that are important to consider for children with externalizing behavior will be reviewed. The second purpose of this article is to present screening and intervention strategies that school psychologists may use with young children who have externalizing behavior prior to or as soon as they enter the kindergarten setting.

Characteristics of Children at Risk

Early behavior patterns. A prospective longitudinal study found that children who were rated as having externalizing problems when they were 7 years old were rated by their mothers as

---

Correspondence to: Dr. Melissa Stormont, Department of Special Education, University of Missouri–Columbia, 310 Townsend, Columbia, MO 65211.

having more difficult temperaments as early as when they were infants (Sanson, Smart, Prior, & Oberklaid, 1993). Thus, for preschool children with difficult behavior, certain temperamental characteristics in infancy, such as colic and excessive crying, may be important to consider. Maternal ratings of difficult temperament when children were 3 years old have also been documented to be a strong predictor of behavior problems when children were 9 years old (Egeland et al., 1990). Other researchers have similarly found that more specific preschool temperament characteristics including activity (Barron & Earls, 1984; Sanson et al., 1993), withdrawal, intensity, negative mood, problems adapting, inflexibility (Barron & Earls, 1984), reactivity, irritability, low persistence (Sanson et al., 1993), and more difficulty managing behavior (Campbell, Szumowski, Ewing, Gluck, & Breaux, 1982; Sanson et al., 1993) have been differentially associated with children with externalizing behavior problems. Finally, in recent research, Stormont (in press) documented that preschool children with stable behavior problems were more active and intense than children who showed improved behavior at outcome and comparisons.

Although temperamental characteristics are important early risk factors, it is important to stress that they alone do not strongly predict externalizing outcomes (Webster-Stratton, 1997). Children's temperament characteristics (e.g., intensity, irritability) appear to interact with other child and family characteristics to predict outcomes. For example, children with both hyperactivity and aggression were more irritable and reactive than children with hyperactivity when they were 3 years old (Sanson et al., 1993). Thus, not surprisingly, children with both hyperactivity and aggression had more difficult temperaments than children with only hyperactivity. These children also appear to be at greatest risk for future problems.

Research has clearly found that children with both hyperactivity and aggression are at greater risk for future behavior problems than children with either hyperactivity or aggression (e.g., Speltz, McClellan, DeKlyen, & Jones, 1999; Stormont, 2000). According to their fathers, preschoolers with hyperactivity and aggression were more likely than preschoolers with hyperactivity or comparisons to have externalizing problems 5 years later (Stormont, 2000). Other research has found that up to 67% of children with both hyperactivity and aggression in their preschool years continued to have severe behavior problems at age 9 (Campbell & Ewing, 1990). Similar research has found that preschool children with a dual diagnosis of attention-deficit hyperactivity disorder (ADHD) and oppositional defiant disorder (ODD) were more likely than children with only ODD to have a disorder at a 2-year follow-forward (Speltz et al., 1999).

In addition to evaluating the type of externalizing behavior and temperament characteristics when determining children's risk for stable externalizing behavior problems, it is also important to consider other factors such as age, gender, severity, pervasiveness, and stability of behavior problems (Campbell, 1998; Webster-Stratton, 1997). Clearly, it is important to consider the age of the child when determining risk for developmental reasons. Noncompliant behavior in toddlers should be evaluated differently than oppositional behavior in 4-year-olds (Campbell, 1998). Furthermore, it is important to determine risk based on multiple problem behaviors that occur in multiple settings (Campbell, 1998; Webster-Stratton, 1997). According to Campbell, "Isolated behaviors in and of themselves do not determine whether or not a disorder exists" (p. 8). In addition, Campbell reported that gender differences in externalizing behavior appear to be less prevalent in preschoolers. However, research that has investigated gender and specific types of externalizing behavior has documented some significant differences. Specifically, one study found that preschool children of varying ages (i.e., 3–5 years) differed on three externalizing subscales with boys scoring higher than girls (i.e., conduct problems, hyperactivity, hyperactivity index; Miller, Koplewicz, & Klein, 1997). However, when analyzed by age, no gender differences were found for 3- and 5-year-olds on the conduct problem subscale. Three-, 4-, and 5-year-old boys had higher ratings on both the hyperactivity and the hyperactivity index than same-aged girls.

Finally, in the identification process, it is relevant to consider that certain children are at greater risk for behavior problems due to poverty. Research has found that, according to teachers, children in Head Start settings were rated as more physically aggressive (i.e., hitting, kicking, pushing, shoving, grabbing) than a random sample of comparison preschoolers (Kupersmidt, Bryant, & Willoughby, 2000). However, this research also found that preschoolers in the comparison group were rated by teachers as engaging in more name calling or teasing than children in the Head Start setting. Boys were rated as more aggressive than girls on many specific types of aggression (i.e., hitting, arguing). Overall, boys engaged in daily antisocial aggression at rates three times that of the girls. Other research found that boys in Head Start classrooms had higher parent-ratings of externalizing behavior problems than girls (Kaiser, Hancock, Cai, Foster, & Hester, 2000).

In summary, many characteristics should be considered when determining which children are most in need of early intervention. From the research it is clear that early externalizing behavior patterns that include hyperactivity, aggression, challenging temperament characteristics, and poverty place children at greater risk for developing or sustaining behavior problems. Young boys may be more likely to exhibit externalizing behavior problems than girls. As indicated previously, assessment of these child characteristics in isolation is not sufficient to determine children's risk for stable behavior problems. Professionals also need to consider family and school contexts that may interact with a challenging child's behavior to produce poor outcomes and/or contribute to the development of challenging behavior in young children.

Family characteristics. The research on children with undifferentiated externalizing problems (i.e., hyperactivity and/or aggression) has clearly documented family characteristics that are associated with behavior problems at outcome. Overall, from longitudinal research conducted with preschoolers, the following specific family factors appear to be important predictors of behavior problems in children: marital conflict, maternal depression, low maternal educational level, and family/parenting stress (see Stormont, 1998, for a review). Social support has been documented to be a buffer for families and children (Webster-Stratton, 1997).

Longitudinal research has also been conducted comparing children who improve in their behavior to those who have stable behavior problems. Such research has found that children who continue to have pervasive problems at follow-up had mothers who were initially more depressed, less satisfied with their marriages, and felt more parenting stress than mothers of children who had transient behavior problems or comparisons (Campbell, 1994). A 5-year longitudinal study found that children with stable behavior problems had, as preschoolers, mothers who reported having lower educational levels, using greater levels of control in their child rearing, and having greater marital conflict than children in the improved behavior group and comparisons (Stormont, in press).

From the research reviewed thus far, it can be speculated that children's characteristics interact with their families' to produce and sustain children's behavior problems. Research indeed supports this type of interaction. That is, children with more severe behavior problems appear to have more stressors in their families. In one study, preschool children with both hyperactivity and aggression had families who had more adverse characteristics than preschoolers with only hyperactivity (Stormont-Spurgin & Zentall, 1995). Moffitt (1990) has also found that adolescents with the most severe adolescent outcomes (both delinquency and ADD) had more family adversity when they were preschoolers than youth with single disorders. Researchers have described children at greatest risk for having behavior problems as those who "do not have either the internal resources or the external supports to help them overcome early difficulties with self-regulation and behavior control" (Campbell, Pierce, March, Ewing, & Szumowski, 1994, p. 837).

Thus, young children with both hyperactivity and aggression and family adversity may indeed lack both the internal and external resources to avoid maintaining and/or developing more serious behavior problems. One external resource that is particularly important for these young children is the manner in which their parents manage their challenging behavior. Research has clearly illuminated the importance of parent–child interactions in families with challenging children. A review of this research follows.

Parent–child interactions. It is clear from the research that there is a strong relationship between early harsh management by parents and children's aggression (Webster-Stratton, 1997). The association between parental aggression toward children and their social outcomes at school has also been investigated. Research has found that parental aggression toward children at home was differentially associated with children's sociometric groups in kindergarten (Strassberg, Dodge, Bates, & Pettit, 1992). This research also found that parental aggression toward the child at home contributed significant predictive power to children's social status at school above and beyond the variance accounted for by children's aggression at school.

Research has also clearly documented that negative and controlling types of parenting place children at risk for developing or sustaining behavior problems. Research has found that observed maternal negative control during an observation with their children when they were 3 years old was predictive of antisocial behavior and discipline problems when their children were 9 years old (Campbell & Ewing, 1990). Similarly, Stormont (2001) found that children with more stable behavior problems had mothers who self-reported greater maternal control in child rearing when children were preschoolers than mothers of children who had improved and comparisons. In addition to determining that controlling and aggressive types of child rearing or discipline styles are associated with externalizing behavior and stable behavior problems, it is also important to understand the qualitative dynamics of the interactions that young children with externalizing behavior have with their parents. Research has been conducted to further describe the interactions between mothers and their children with conduct problems.

Gardner (1987, 1989) investigated the interactions of mothers and their preschoolers with conduct problems. Gardner (1987) documented that mothers and children with conduct problems spent 20% of their time in negative interactions (12.3 minutes per hour), which is a rate almost 10 times that of mothers and children without conduct problems (2.6 minutes per hour). Furthermore, children with conduct problems spent more time doing nothing or watching TV; children without conduct problems spent more time playing alone. Comparisons also spent over twice as much time as children with conduct problems engaged in positive interactions with their mothers. Gardner (1989) further investigated the interaction styles of mothers and their children with conduct problems and documented that mothers and children with conduct problems spent a greater amount of time engaged in angry conflict (6.5 minutes per hour) than did comparisons (.4 minutes per hour). Additionally, in the dyads with children with conduct problems, mothers were not consistent after issuing a command. In fact, 67% of the time mothers gave a command they did not follow through and solicit compliance from their child.

Classroom Factors

Teacher interactions. No research could be located on interactions between preschoolers with externalizing problems and their teachers. However, research has been conducted with older children with behavior problems and their interactions with teachers. Interestingly, the amount of time spent in negative and positive interactions between teachers and students with behavior problems parallels the research on mother–child interactions. Specifically, teachers spent more than 20% of the time in negative interactions with students with behavior disorders and less than

5% of the time engaged in positive interactions with such students (Jack et al., 1996). Even though teachers have been found to be engaged in four times as many negative to positive interactions with these youth, other research has documented that the occurrence of aggression and noncompliance in children with behavior problems was relatively low and that children typically comply with teacher directives (Gunter & Coutinho, 1997).

Unfortunately, when students with behavior problems do comply or demonstrate appropriate behavior, teachers may not consistently reinforce their behavior. That is, research has documented that teachers of students with aggressive behavior did not attend to their students' hand raising behavior at high rates. Specifically, teachers of students with aggressive behavior who were in integrated classroom settings responded to students' hand raises approximately 20% of the time (Shores et al., 1993).

Other research has investigated the different interactions between teachers and students rated in the high-risk or mid-risk range for aggressive behavior (Van Acker, Grant, & Henry, 1996). Lag sequential analysis was used to determine whether certain antecedents were associated with higher conditional probabilities of being followed by another event than would be expected (i.e., the unconditional probability). Interestingly, teacher behavior appeared to be different depending on children's risk status. Specifically, for children at mid risk for aggression, children's volunteering behavior predicted having an opportunity to respond, which in turn predicted giving a correct response, which then predicted the receipt of praise. In addition, negative behavior predicted the receipt of a reprimand or redirection. For children at high risk for aggression, a more concerning interaction pattern was documented. That is, volunteering behavior for this group did not lead to higher probabilities (than chance) for having an opportunity to respond. Also, giving a correct response did not predict teacher praise for these children. Teachers also did not use redirection as a response for negative behavior; teachers used reprimands for negative behavior with high-risk students, which in turn set the occasion for more noncompliant behavior.

Given low rates of positive interactions with teachers and reinforcement for appropriate behavior, it is important that professionals work with teachers to help them support and respond to students in a manner that increases positive behavior and reduces inappropriate behavior (Gunter & Coutinho, 1997). It is also important that professionals working with teachers on behavior management skills understand what the research has documented in regard to teachers' intervention preferences.

Teacher intervention preferences. A recent study investigated preschool teachers' ratings for 43 supportive educational interventions for students with ADHD (Stormont & Stebbins, 2001). Teachers were asked to rate each item based on their perceptions of both the importance of the intervention and their comfort implementing the intervention. Although this research did not measure whether teachers felt the same interventions were as important for any preschool student or for those with general externalizing behavior, it is worth reviewing in this article as it provides some information regarding preschool teachers' perceptions of the importance of using supportive interventions. Overall, it was documented that preschool teachers rated the majority of the interventions as either mostly or extremely important and rated their comfort levels in the moderately comfortable to totally comfortable range. Teacher variables, including years of teaching experience, educational level, and having a child with ADHD in their classroom, were not related to importance or comfort ratings.

What was not investigated in this research was whether teachers were implementing or had actually implemented the interventions. However, it is worth noting that preschool teachers did not rate any of the interventions as unimportant and did not report that they would feel uncomfortable using any of the strategies. These data are encouraging since many of the intervention strategies were behavior management techniques that would also be important to implement with preschoolers with externalizing behavior including, for example, using proximity, praise, planned ignoring, and cues for appropriate behavior.

Other research has also investigated the behavior management preferences of teachers (85% of sample) and other professionals (15%) who worked with children aged preschool through high school (Alderman & Nix, 1997). This study found that, overall, professionals rated strategies for increasing behavior such as using a point system, designing contracts, and sending a positive note home to parents more positively than strategies for decreasing behavior (i.e., removal from activity, negative note home to parents, and loss of privileges). Teachers with more years of experience had higher ratings for interventions to increase behavior than teachers with less experience. Severity of the problem behavior was not associated with intervention preferences.

Screening

Children with externalizing behavior need intervention to support the development of and/or production of more appropriate social behavior. Many factors need to be considered before designing a social skills curriculum or a behavior management program for a student(s). First, professionals must select a screening method. Professionals could screen children for risk based on the previous characteristics. However, it is important to emphasize that screening to identify children with externalizing behavior is an area that should be addressed in a sensitive manner with other professionals and parents. Webster-Stratton (1997) discussed the importance of identifying preschool children who need intervention and, at the same time, cautioned professionals to be weary of attaching disorder labels to young children. Another recommended option, which reflects a more developmentally appropriate way to screen for externalizing behavior, is to use standardized behavior rating scales (Webster-Stratton, 1997).

Researchers have recently documented another way to screen young children for disruptive behavior problems (Barkley et al., 2000). In this study, screening took place in an urban setting and participants were predominantly from low-income families. Parents were asked to a complete brief behavior screening scale, which took a total of 10 minutes or less to complete. Children who scored high (i.e., 93rd percentile) on both conduct problems and hyperactive-impulsive behavior items were solicited for participation in the study and randomly assigned to one of four conditions. The results of this study and the effective treatment components are discussed in the intervention section.

Finally, another strategy that could be used in any preschool setting includes implementing a validated early screening method designed for the prevention of emotional and behavior disorders in young children (Walker, Colvin, & Ramsey, 1995). The Early Screening Project (ESP) involves screening classrooms of children and includes three stages. In the first stage, teachers are asked to rank the students in their classroom in terms of the presence of internalizing and externalizing behavior problems. The three top-ranking students for internalizing and externalizing behavior problems pass through the first phase of screening. The second phase or stage of screening includes teacher ratings for the top internalizers and externalizers (a total of 6 children). The authors stress that, although teachers have to complete multiple ratings scales, the number of students is small as teachers are only completing rating scales on students at high risk. Students who meet the specified criteria for stage two ratings go to the final stage of assessment. Stage three assessments include direct observations of students in multiple settings.

Interventions

Prior to the presentation of best practice strategies for children with externalizing behavior it is important to address the importance of establishing supportive relationships with teachers and parents for maintenance of improved behavior and generalization of skills. It is important that many factors be considered when designing collaborative relationships with teachers. It is obvious that teachers need to have more than a workshop on working with challenging behavior. From the research reviewed in this article it is clear that teachers may need more support implementing techniques, such as specific behavior praise, that they do not use at high rates. To support teachers use of behavior management strategies, Lewis and Sugai (1999) recommend that professionals draw from the knowledge base related to what motivates teachers in the change process. For example, teachers need to be provided ongoing support in the process of learning new skills, and they need frequent feedback on students' outcomes.

It is also important to establish collaborative relationships with families of children with externalizing problems. As previously discussed, many times children with externalizing problems are in family contexts that include stress, marital conflict, and parents who use controlling and perhaps harsh discipline. This information is important to school professionals when determining which children are at risk for behavior problems. However, in addition to contributing to a calculation of risk for children, this information could also inform and stimulate outreach efforts. It is clear that this process may be challenging if families are not actively seeking assistance. One option to support reinforcement of children's adaptive behavior at home is to implement interventions in school that include home components. Many examples of such components are presented in the following sections. The following interventions include interventions that a school psychologist or early childhood professional could implement with children with externalizing behavior. The interventions are organized in terms of classwide interventions and more individualized types of interventions.

Classwide. Prior to working with individual children in a classroom setting, it is important to determine if classwide supports for desired behavior are present (Sugai & Lewis, 1996). Classroom supports for positive student behavior include establishing, for example, positive teacher–student interactions, clear classroom rules that are taught, posted, and consistently reviewed and enforced, less wait time for students, smooth transitions, and a positive environment that includes structure and routines (Jones & Jones, 1998; Walker et al., 1995).

Another important component to effective classroom management is to provide clear instruction in the area of social skills. There are many factors to consider when designing and implementing a social skills curriculum. First, it is critical to determine who needs social skills instruction (Sugai & Lewis, 1996). Next, it is important to determine the skills that need to be addressed in order to guide the selection of an appropriate social skills curriculum (for a more thorough review of social skills assessment considerations including purposes and types of assessments, see Sugai & Lewis, 1996). Once target social skills have been determined, it is important to design social skills instruction to reflect effective teaching practices for learning any new skill. One format that has been supported for use in social skills instruction is the model-lead-test format, which includes eight key components. First, the social skill is clearly named (e.g., asking for help). Next, a critical rule is provided to help the student(s) determine when the skill should be used. This component is critical for children who have difficulty producing appropriate skills in context. For example, perhaps a student, Jon, is working on "asking for help" in an appropriate way. Jon almost always gets frustrated during art but does not ask for help. Instead, he gets up, throws his chair, and is removed from art. Jon could be prompted to demonstrate the critical rule for asking for help before he goes to art. This would help the student discriminate contexts where he could and probably would need to produce the target skill.

The next components of a good lesson plan are to provide the specific skill components and to model the skill components. Sugai and Lewis (1996) stress the importance of using demonstrations that are both age-appropriate and reflective of the environment of the students. Both appropriate and inappropriate examples that are representative of realistic situations should be presented by competent and respected individuals. Students are then provided opportunities to practice the skill in role-play situations and given corrective feedback and positive reinforcement. At this point in the instruction, it is important that students practice only the examples of the correct execution of the target social skill.

Finally, students are provided with review opportunities, tested on their knowledge and use of the skill in context, and provided opportunities for practicing the skill through homework assignments. There are multiple social skills curricula for professionals to use as a starting place. However, professionals should remember that most curricula would need to be modified to be more sensitive to students' needs and lives (Sugai & Lewis, 1996).

Intensive interventions.   Many children with behavior problems will need more intensive and individualized interventions. This section will include some examples of more intensive and systematic interventions for children who need more support. First, a classroom behavior management intervention that was recently documented to be effective for kindergartners will be reviewed. Next, two programs that have been empirically supported for use with children with behavior problems will be described. The last strategy presented is functional behavior assessment, a strategy that is the most individualized and should be employed whenever possible and particularly when other more generalized intervention programs fail.

In a recent study, kindergarten children who were in a school-based intervention condition (with or without combined parent training) differed significantly from the parent-training and control groups on outcome measures at the end of the kindergarten school year (Barkley et al., 2000). Specifically, children in the classroom intervention groups had lower teacher ratings of aggression, attention problems, and behavior problems and lower externalizing behavior scores than children in the parent training or comparison groups. Students receiving the classroom intervention were also rated by their teachers as having better social skills and more adaptive behavior at home than students who did not receive the classroom treatment. The classroom intervention consisted of numerous behavior interventions including token-economies, response cost, time out, and overcorrection. Students were also taught skills through group training in social skills, self-control techniques (cognitive-behavior), and anger management. In addition, individual support in specific settings was given as needed.

Thus, the classroom intervention for these kindergartners combined skill building with systematic consequences for appropriate and inappropriate behavior. The need for more intensive interventions for specific children in the classroom setting has also led to the development and subsequent field testing of specific programs. The following programs involve intensive support in the beginning of the program in the form of a trained person who initially provides the intervention.

First Step to Success is a program that involves implementing (a) systematic screening to determine children at risk for antisocial behavior, (b) school interventions for teaching and supporting adaptive behavior, and (c) collaboration between teachers and parents in supporting adaptive skills (Walker, 1998). A program consultant receives up to 60 hours of training in the First Step modules and components prior to implementing the program with a student (Walker, 1998).

After a child is selected for the program, a trained First Step consultant initiates the program in the child's classroom. The consultant implements a specialized program (i.e., The School Intervention Module), arranges rewards and contingent free-time activities for students, and collaborates with parents on their implementation of the home components of the program and their child's progress at school. The program includes successful completion of 30 program days. There is a specific performance criterion that has to be met each day prior to proceeding to the next day.

Since many of the program days have to be repeated, most children required at least 2 months to complete the program. The first part of the module involves using a point card and marking green when the student is performing the desired behavior and marking red when the student is not. Initially, the intervals are small (30 seconds) to allow for opportunities for more reinforcement. Also, if children have desired behavior in 80% of the intervals for a session (typically two each day), then they receive a free-time activity with peers. If children meet the criterion for both sessions that day, they also receive a reward at home.

Over time, the cards are faded and a leaner schedule of reinforcement is instituted. The next phase involves the teacher taking over the program with ongoing support and communication with the consultant. More specifically, the teacher takes over the point system, provision of positive praise, organization of the free-time activities, and the school- and home-based rewards. In the last phase of the program, points are replaced with more natural reinforcers such as teacher praise and recognition from parents.

Parents are an integral part of this program. Perhaps the success of the First Step program over time, without boosters, can be attributed to the sustained reinforcement of desired skills by parents in the home. While the School Intervention Module is being implemented in the child's classroom, the First Step consultant makes six 60-minute in-home visits to present lessons on target skills in different areas (e.g., Cooperation). The program contains specific instructional guidelines, activities, and games that parents can play with their child to build competence in the target skills. The First Step program can be purchased as a kit with prepared materials for both the school and home programs (Walker, 1998).

The second program has also been designed for use in the general education classroom. However, rather than being designed for students with early antisocial behavior patterns, the Irvine Paraprofessional Program (IPP) was initially designed to support the needs of children with ADHD (Kotkin, 1998). Even though the IPP was originally designed to support students with ADHD, the components are based on best practice for children with externalizing behavior, which is why it is presented in this article. The program was designed to be implemented by a paraprofessional under the supervision of a school psychologist. The paraprofessionals receive extensive training, including 30 hours of coursework designed to cover seven modules. In addition, paraprofessionals also participate in a 200-hour supervised field experience in the general education classroom. Paraprofessionals who meet competency requirements are placed for half days (typically mornings) in a classroom with a child with ADHD. The goal or desired outcome of the program is to modify a child's behavior through the use of effective classroom and behavior management techniques such as establishing and enforcing classroom rules, modifying assignments, using continuous reinforcement, using group contingencies, and using techniques to decrease inappropriate behavior. In addition, the paraprofessional implements a point system for part of the day for 12 weeks.

As with the First Step program, the target child begins with more frequent feedback, with points and praise awarded to the child every 15 minutes. Children can turn in their points for a child-selected activity at the end of the day. Over time, the teacher takes over the responsibility of the program and provides the points and reinforcement. This program also includes teaching the target child how to use self-management and social skills instruction. The paraprofessional conducts social skills lessons twice a week in a pull-out format and then provides prompts and reinforcement for using the target skills in context. Overall, both the First Step program and the IPP have promising empirical data to support their use with students with externalizing disorders (Kotkin, 1998; Walker, Stiller, Severson, Golly, & Feil, 1998). However, some children do not benefit from these programs and require more individually tailored interventions. Another technique that is more individualized is functional behavior assessment.

Experts in the area of functional behavior assessment (FBA) define FBA as "a systematic process of identifying problem behaviors and the events that (a) reliably predict occurrences and non-occurrence of those behaviors and (b) maintain the behaviors across time" (OSEP Center on Positive Behavioral Interventions and Support, 1999, p. 12). If professionals can identify the conditions that surround the problem behavior then environments can be modified to reduce problem behavior and replacement behavior can be taught and systematically reinforced. FBA is a process used to develop an understanding of behavior in order to develop relevant and efficient interventions. At a minimum, experts in this area recommend that an FBA yield three results. First, hypothesis statements should be generated and should include an operational definition of the target problem behavior (or behaviors), the antecedent conditions that are reliably associated with the target behavior, and the consequences that appear to maintain the behavior. Second, it is important that objective observational data are collected to support the hypotheses. Finally, a behavior support plan needs to be written to address strategies for changing setting events, antecedents, and consequences. In addition, the support plan should address the specific alternative behavior that needs to be taught and reinforced to replace the inappropriate behavior.

Summary

In summary, it is important that children at high risk for externalizing problems are identified and then provided early intervention. Accordingly the two main purposes of this article were to (a) review the characteristics of children who are at increased risk for developing and/or maintaining externalizing behavior patterns, and (b) provide options for intervening with these young children. It is critical that more behavior screening and early intervention efforts are constructed and systematically implemented within preschool and kindergarten classrooms. These efforts are especially important for children with early behavior problems who are also in adverse home environments, as school may be a buffer against the development of more severe problems. According to Kaiser and Hester (1997), "When parents are unskilled in managing their children's behavior or when the environment is particularly impoverished or stressful, children are likely to need intensive school-based support to successfully negotiate the early school years" (p. 125).

REFERENCES

Alderman, G.L., & Nix, M. (1997). Teachers' intervention preferences related to explanations for behavior problems, severity of the problem, and teacher experience. Behavior Disorders, 22, 87–95.

Barkley, R.A., Shelton, T.L., Crosswait, C., Moorehouse, M., Fletcher, K., Barrett, S., Jenkins, L., & Metevia, L. (2000). Multi-method psycho-educational intervention for preschool children with disruptive behavior: Preliminary results at post-treatment. Journal of Child Psychology, Psychiatry, and Allied Disciplines, 41, 319–332.

Barron, A.P., & Earls, F. (1984). The relation of temperament and social factors to behavior problems in three-year-old children. Journal of Child Psychology and Psychiatry, 25, 23–33.

Campbell, S.B. (1994). Hard-to-manage preschool boys: Externalizing behavior, social competence, and family context at two-year follow-up. Journal of Abnormal Child Psychology, 22, 147–166.

Campbell, S.B. (1998). Developmental perspectives. In T.H. Ollendick & M. Hersen (Eds.), Handbook of child psychopathology (3rd ed., pp. 3–35). New York: Plenum Press.

Campbell, S.B., & Ewing, L.J. (1990). Follow-up of hard to manage preschoolers: Adjustment at age 9 and predictors of continuing symptoms. Journal of Child Psychology and Psychiatry, 31, 871–889.

Campbell, S.B., Pierce, E.W., March, C.L., Ewing, L.J., & Szumowski, E.K. (1994). Hard-to-manage preschool boys: Symptomatic behavior across contexts and time. Child Development, 65, 836–851.

Campbell, S.B., Szumowski, E.K., Ewing, L.J., Gluck, D.S., & Breaux, A.M. (1982). A multidimensional assessment of parent-identified behavior problem toddlers. Journal of Abnormal Child Psychology, 10, 569–592.

Egeland, B., Kalkoske, M., Gottesman, N., & Erickson, M.F. (1990). Preschool behavior problems: Stability and factors accounting for change. Journal of Child Psychology and Psychiatry, 31, 891–909.

Gardner, F.E.M. (1987). Positive interaction between mothers and conduct problem children: Is there training for harmony as well as for fighting? Journal of Abnormal Child Psychology, 15, 283–293.

Gardner, F.E.M. (1989). Inconsistent parenting: Is there evidence for a link with children's conduct problems? Journal of Abnormal Child Psychology, 17, 223–233.

Gunter, P.L., & Coutinho, M.J. (1997). Negative reinforcement in classrooms: What we're beginning to learn. Teacher Education and Special Education, 20, 249–264.

Jack, S.L., Shores, R.E., Denny, R.K., Gunter, P.L., DeBriere, T., & DePaepe, P. (1996). An analysis of the relationship of teachers' reported use of classroom management strategies on types of classroom interactions. The Journal of Behavioral Education, 6, 67–87.

Jones, V.F., & Jones, L.S. (1998). Comprehensive classroom management: Creating communities of support and solving problems (5th ed.). Boston: Allyn and Bacon.

Kaiser, A.P., Hancock, T.B., Cai, X., Foster, E.M., & Hester, P.P. (2000). Parent-reported behavioral problems and language delays in boys and girls enrolled in Head Start classrooms. Behavior Disorders, 26, 26–41.

Kaiser, A.P., & Hester, P.P. (1997). Prevention of conduct disorder through early intervention: A social-communicative perspective. Behavior Disorders, 22, 117–130.

Kotkin, R. (1998). The Irvine paraprofessional program: Promising practice for serving students with ADHD. Journal of Learning Disabilities, 31, 556–564.

Kupersmidt, J.B., Bryant, D., & Willoughby, M.T. (2000). Prevalence of aggressive behaviors among preschoolers in head start and community child care programs. Behavior Disorders, 26, 42–52.

Lewis, T.J., & Sugai, G. (1999). Effective behavior support: A systems approach to proactive schoolwide management. Focus on Exceptional Children, 31, 1–24.

Miller, L.S., Koplewicz, H.S., & Klein, R.G. (1997). Teacher ratings of hyperactivity, inattention, and conduct problems in preschoolers. Journal of Abnormal Psychology, 25, 113–119.

Moffitt, T. (1990). Juvenile delinquency and attention deficit disorder: Boys' developmental trajectories from age 3 to age 15. Child Development, 61, 893–910.

OSEP Center on Positive Behavioral Interventions and Support. (1999, August). Applying positive behavioral support and functional behavioral assessment in schools (Technical Assistance Guide No. 1.4.3).

Sanson, A., Smart, D., Prior, M., & Oberklaid, F. (1993). Precursors of hyperactivity and aggression. Journal of the American Academy of Child and Adolescent Psychiatry, 32, 1207–1216.

Shores, R.E., Jack, S.L., Gunter, P.L., Ellis, D.N., DeBriere, T.J., & Wehby, J.H. (1993). Classroom interactions of children with behavior disorders. Journal of Emotional and Behavioral Disorders, 1, 27–39.

Speltz, M.L., McClellan, J., DeKlyen, M., & Jones, K. (1999). Preschool boys with oppositional defiant disorder: Clinical presentation and diagnostic change. Journal of the American Academy of Child and Adolescent Psychiatry, 38, 838–845.

Stormont, M. (1998). Family factors associated with externalizing disorders in preschoolers. Journal of Early Intervention, 21, 323–251.

Stormont, M. (2000). Early child risk factors for externalizing and internalizing behavior at a five year follow-forward assessment. Journal of Early Intervention, 23, 180–190.

Stormont, M. (in press). Family and child characteristics associated with stable behavior problems in preschool children. Manuscript submitted for publication.

Stormont, M., & Stebbins, M. (2001). Preschool teachers' accommodation preferences for children with AD/HD. Psychology in the Schools, 38, 259–268.

Stormont-Spurgin, M., & Zentall, S.S. (1995). Contributing factors in the manifestation of aggression in preschoolers with hyperactivity. Journal of Child Psychology, Psychiatry, and Allied Disciplines, 36, 491–509.

Strassberg, Z., Dodge, K.A., Bates, J.E., & Pettit, G.S. (1992). The longitudinal relation between parental conflict strategies and children's sociometric standing in kindergarten. Merrill-Palmer Quarterly, 38, 477–493.

Sugai, G., & Lewis, T.J. (1996). Preferred and promising practices for social skills instruction. Focus on Exceptional Children, 29, 1–16.

Van Acker, R., Grant, S.H., & Henry, D. (1996). Teacher and student behavior as a function of risk for aggression. Education and Treatment of Children, 19, 316–334.

Vitaro, F., Tremblay, R.E., Gagnon, C., & Biovin, M. (1992). Peer rejection from kindergarten to grade 2: Outcomes, correlates, and prediction. Merrill-Palmer Quarterly, 38, 382–400.

Vitaro, F., Tremblay, R.E., Gagnon, C., & Pelletier, D. (1994). Predictive accuracy of behavioral and sociometric assessments of high-risk kindergarten children. Journal of Clinical Child Psychology, 23, 272–282.

Walker, H.M. (1998, March/April). First steps to prevent antisocial behavior. Teaching Exceptional Children, 16–19.

Walker, H.M., Colvin, G., & Ramsey, E. (1995). Antisocial behavior in school: Strategies and best practices. Pacific Grove, CA: Brooks/Cole.

Walker, H.M., Stiller, B., Severson, H.H., Golly, A., & Feil, E.G. (1998). First step to success: Intervening at the point of school entry to prevent antisocial behavior patterns. Psychology in the Schools, 35, 259–269.

Webster-Stratton, C. (1997). Early intervention for families of preschool children with conduct problems. In M.J. Guralnick (Ed.), The effectiveness of early intervention (pp. 429–453). Baltimore, MD: Brookes.

White, J.L., Moffitt, T.E., Earls, F., Robins, L., & Silva, P.A. (1990). How early can we tell?: Predictors of childhood conduct disorder and adolescent delinquency. Criminology, 28, 507–533.

Psychology in the Schools, Vol. 39(2), 2002
© 2002 Wiley Periodicals, Inc.

DOI: 10.1002/pits.10026

MULTIFACETED FUNCTIONAL BEHAVIOR ASSESSMENT FOR STUDENTS WITH EXTERNALIZING BEHAVIOR DISORDERS

DANIEL E. OLYMPIA, LORA TUESDAY HEATHFIELD, WILLIAM R. JENSON,

AND ELAINE CLARK

University of Utah

Recent federal mandates have increased interest in the use of functional behavior assessment as a necessary part of initial and ongoing work with students with externalizing behavior disorders. A multifaceted approach to functional behavior assessment provides a comprehensive assessment of both behavioral excesses and deficits commonly found in externalizing behavior disorders and also provides for the linkage of assessment information to educational interventions that can be implemented and monitored in educational settings for students with behavior disorders. The authors, using a variety of empirically derived methods, describe specific components of a multifaceted approach to functional behavior assessment in the context of the widely accepted behavioral excess/deficit model for students with externalizing behavior disorders. Empirically derived and validated methodologies (i.e., indirect data collection and analysis, direct observation and recording of behavior, and use of probes to establish baseline rates and measure impacts of intervention) are described. Technology-assisted data collection and analysis using computer-assisted functional behavior assessment interviews and direct observation of behavior using personal digital assistant (PDA) based software are also presented as a means to improve efficiency and reduce time needed to conduct adequate functional behavior assessments. Specific strategies to address academic skill and performance deficits as well as social skills deficiencies in the context of a multifaceted functional behavior assessment are also presented for students with externalizing behavior disorders. © 2002 Wiley Periodicals, Inc.

Functional behavior assessment procedures are not new and have a long history in psychology, with well-established roots in applied behavior analysis (Bijou, Peterson, & Ault, 1968; Skinner, 1953). Skinner describes lawful cause and effect relationships in behavior between stimulus-controlling events and the consequences that follow. Sidman's (1960) work with single-case design further advanced the experimental analysis of behavior and its relationship to controlling environmental events. Other major advances in functional behavior assessment came as a response to problems such as self-injurious behavior where observations were made of an individual's behavior in direct response to the systematic manipulation of environmental conditions (Iwata et al., 1982/1994). With this form of functional behavior assessment, hypotheses were generated and tested using direct manipulation of antecedent and consequence events. However, other forms of functional behavior assessment have also been introduced which include behavioral interviews and archival record review (O'Neill, Horner, Albin, Storey, & Sprague, 1997), behavior rating scales (Durand & Crimmins, 1988), and direct observation of the behavior in an environment in which it is likely to occur (Ellingson, Miltenberger, & Long, 1999). With these approaches, antecedent and consequences events are not manipulated but rather assessed using indirect and direct methods.

The process of functional behavior assessment has focused on determining the environmental variables that set the occasion for, and maintain problem behaviors. Functional behavior assessment procedures can be classed into three broad categories: indirect (interview and record review), direct (observation), and experimental manipulations (probes) (Lennox & Miltenberger, 1989). The trade-offs between these procedures include ease of information collection through retrospective interviewing and record review as opposed to the more laborious and time-intensive direct observation and experimental manipulation. However, the more direct forms of functional behavior

Correspondence to: Daniel E. Olympia, University of Utah, 1705 E. Campus Center Drive, Room 327, Salt Lake City, UT 84112. E-mail: Olympia@ed.utah.edu

assessment may provide information that is more valid as they do not rely on memories of informants or information collected from records. For students with externalizing behavior disorders in time-sensitive educational environments, there is a place for both indirect and direct methods as well as brief experimental manipulations when conducting functional behavior assessments.

Although as a group, students with externalizing behavior disorders differ considerably in terms of their learning histories, skill levels, skill deficits, and presenting behavior concerns, these students share some general characteristics that lend themselves to a functional behavior assessment paradigm. These characteristics include behavioral excesses such as noncompliance, aggression, arguing, property destruction, and disruptive behaviors (Gelfand, Jenson, & Drew, 1997; Patterson, Reid, & Dishion, 1992; Rhode, Jenson, & Reavis, 1992). Other behavioral excesses such as fire-setting, animal abuse, sexual perpetration, and aggression may be more covert, occur less frequently, and have varying degrees of intensity. Students with externalizing behavior disorders also exhibit behavioral deficits such as limited on-task behavior, problematic self-management skills, poor social skills, and significant academic deficiencies (Barkley, 1998; Dishion, Andrews, & Crosby, 1995, Hinshaw, 1992; Hinshaw & Anderson, 1996). Often these behaviors are observed at higher rates of occurrence and lower intensities, but they also have significant cumulative impacts over time. Students with externalizing behavior disorders who cannot perform the required academic and social tasks in a classroom because of their behavioral deficits, commonly exhibit behavioral excesses to escape that environment.

Existing research and development of functional behavior assessment procedures has focused on self-injury and aggressive behaviors with individuals who have severe developmental disabilities (Hartwig, 2000; Iwata et al., 1982/1994; McComas, Hoch, & Mace, 2000; Repp & Karsh, 1994). Functional behavior assessment procedures applied to individuals with mild-to-moderate disabilities (e.g., students with externalizing behavior disorders in educational settings) are relatively new and lag behind more established applications with developmental disability populations in clinic or institutional settings. However, the re-authorization of the Individuals with Disabilities Education Act (IDEA) Amendments of 1997 (Public Law 105–17) specifically requires that a functional behavior assessment must be conducted for students with disabilities when (a) the student has engaged in a safe school violation (e.g., drugs, weapons, or dangerous behaviors), (b) the student has been suspended for more than 10 days, (c) the student has been subject to expulsion or a change in educational placement, or (d) the student's problematic behavior is a direct manifestation of their disability (Drasgow, Yell, Bradley, & Shriner, 1999). Among students with disabilities in the schools, students with externalizing behavior disorders are far more likely to engage in safe school violations and be subject to suspension or expulsion, thus requiring a functional behavior assessment by law.

In response to these developments, efforts to develop appropriate functional behavior assessment procedures for use with students with externalizing behavior disorders have been initiated (Broussard & Northrup, 1997; Ellingson et al., 2000; Meyer, 1999). These efforts commonly focus on specific problems such as peer attention, teacher attention, curricular issues, or escape from nonpreferred tasks (Broussard & Northrup, 1997), but fail to provide more comprehensive functional behavior assessments, such as those used with developmentally disabled populations. Additionally, many functional behavior analysis procedures have been developed primarily for clinic or institutional use. Their relevance to educational settings may be lacking and their significant time requirements may discourage their use by many educators (Hartwig, 2000). Linking functional behavior assessment results to practical interventions also can be problematic for educators (Hartwig, 2000; Horner, 1994). Most functional behavior assessment systems adequately identify the relationships between the behavior and antecedent and consequence events, but they do not specifically suggest interventions that will be useful in educational settings.

In this article we advocate using a systematic, multifaceted approach to assessing both the behavioral excesses and deficits in students with externalizing behavior disorders using various forms of functional behavior assessment: indirect, direct, and experimental manipulations (probes). Multifaceted functional behavior assessment incorporates indirect interviews and checklists, direct observation of behaviors as well as antecedents and consequences, and when warranted, brief experimental manipulations to assess both the behavioral excesses and behavioral deficits of this population. Technology-assisted data collection and analysis are also highlighted to facilitate ease of use and time efficiency. The focus of this multifaceted approach to functional behavior assessment is to provide a comprehensive assessment of both behavioral excesses and deficits commonly found in students with externalizing behavior disorders. Additional features of this approach necessarily include both time-efficient and practical qualities for educators. Because assessment is inextricably linked to intervention, it is viewed as a process that leads to the development of appropriate interventions and an evaluation of intervention outcomes. Research indicates that treatments clearly linked to functional behavior assessments are more likely to be accepted and implemented by teachers and others in educational settings (Jones & Lungaro, 2000). Therefore, a major emphasis of this multifaceted functional behavior assessment approach is linking assessment information to viable educational interventions that can be used in the classroom for students with externalizing behavior disorders.

FUNCTIONAL BEHAVIOR ASSESSMENT OF BEHAVIORAL EXCESSES

Children and youth with externalizing behavior disorders frequently exhibit disruptive behaviors in a variety of settings including the classroom and less structured school settings, as well as home and community settings. These behavioral excesses are often directed towards the external environment (adults, peers, or property) in the form of noncompliance, tantrums, fighting, arguing, physical or verbal aggression with others as the intended victims (Lochman & Szczepanski, 1999). While behavioral excesses are typically characterized by high frequency of occurrence, long duration and high intensity, various combinations (i.e., low frequency, high intensity and short duration; high frequency, low intensity and long duration, etc.) of these characteristics are also possible (Gelfand, Jenson, & Drew, 1997). A multifaceted approach to functional behavior assessment must anticipate the potential variety and range of these features to appropriately match target behaviors and assessment method.

Systematic Interviewing

Informant reporting through behavioral interviews is one indirect form of functional behavior assessment that is designed to elicit a report of targeted behaviors and related variables by an informant such as a teacher or caregiver. Systematic interviewing formats exist for functional behavior assessments such as the Functional Assessment Interview Format (FAIF) (O'Neill et al., 1997) or the Conducting Functional Behavior Assessments (CFBA) (Nelson, Roberts, & Smith, 1998). While these are useful assessment approaches, validation with students who have externalizing behavior disorders is limited and the time commitments needed to complete each form are substantial. A computer-assisted functional behavior assessment interview, the Functional Assessment and Interventions Program (FAIP; Reavis, Jenson, Morgan, Likins, & Althouse, 1999), was designed specifically for use with students who have externalizing behavior disorders. Information provided by a team of individuals most familiar with the student is entered using a personal computer.

The Functional Assessment and Interventions Program first establishes all relevant information (i.e., a comprehensive medical history, setting information, and pre-existing deficiencies that might affect the selection of interventions for that student). The second component of the FAIP interview prompts for information concerning antecedent factors, which may be influencing the targeted excess behavior. Sample questions in this section address medications, persons, activities, or environmental factors that may precede the target behavior and set the occasion for its occurrence. The third component of the report focuses on consequences that follow the behavior. Questions are asked concerning reactions from staff and peers to the target behavior, access to tangible objects, possible escape or avoidance of particular tasks or environments, or seeking sensory consequences.

After information has been collected on behavioral excesses, antecedents, and consequences, FAIP generates an initial evaluation. The program then prompts for any additional information needed to formulate possible motivations and interventions. The program provides analysis and summary of all entered data and lists a series of research proven intervention strategies that may be used by the team to build an individualized intervention plan. Skill deficiencies, limiting medical concerns, antecedent events, consequences, and confirmed motivations are all used to select the recommended interventions. The interventions list is generally too long to be practically implemented for any one student; rather it serves as a resource to be used by a team to establish an individualized intervention plan.

Preliminary research using FAIP for students with externalizing behavior disorders has been very promising. Test–retest agreement ranged from 73% agreement for all items in the interview to 81% for the motivations section, and inter-rater reliability ranged from 64% agreement for all questions asked by FAIP across two raters for the same student to 71% for FAIP-generated motives (Hartwig, 2000). Concurrent validity was also established between the FAIP (Reavis et al., 1999), the Motivational Assessment Scale (MAS; Durand & Crimmins, 1992), and the Functional Behavior Assessment Interview Form (O'Neill et al., 1997). Using the same student for each pair of raters, percentage of agreement for motives was 69% between the MAS and FAIP and 76% between the FAI and FAIP, indicating good agreement across previously published functional behavior assessment interview formats (Hartwig, 2000).

The Functional Assessment and Interventions Program is a useful interview-based component of a multifaceted functional behavior assessment of students with externalizing behavior disorders with acceptable levels of test–retest reliability and inter-rater reliability and it compares well with other previously published functional behavior assessment systems. Its clear advantage lies in the linkage of functional behavior assessment to interventions suggested by the expert database. The design of an educational program is therefore tailored to the specific abilities, needs, and motives of a student with externalizing behavior disorders. In addition, its time efficiency, ease of use, and understandability to educators makes it a useful part of a multifaceted functional behavior assessment for this population.

Direct Observation

The direct observation of classroom behaviors has been a required component of assessment for students with a variety of identified disabilities. Direct observation of students with externalizing behavior disorders specifically enhances functional behavior assessment by providing actual samples of behavioral excesses in the settings in which the behavior occurs. Research has established that significant differences exist between these types of observable behaviors for children with disabilities and their typical peers, including social and task-oriented behaviors.

For behaviors with proportionately higher rates of occurrence, lower intensity, and longer duration (e.g., off-task, out of seat, talking out, etc.) there are several well-accepted direct observation procedures for use in functional behavior assessment. With direct observation, a rater observes and records a child's performance according to operational definitions of specific targeted behaviors. The practice of observing behaviors of randomly selected peers of the target student has also been used to provide additional criteria for evaluating the context of a behavior as well as the effectiveness of an intervention. Alessi (1980) first described the Response Discrepancy Model goal in terms of reducing the discrepancy between specific problem behaviors and what is considered appropriate in the classroom. The use of on-task observation and response-discrepancy procedures in educational environments (i.e., the classroom or other areas within a school setting) has been well researched and has considerable support (Hartmann, Roper, & Bradford, 1979). Alessi points out that observing the referred student with a comparison student from the same classroom provides school psychologists with a normative framework (i.e., local micro-norms) to compare data obtained from the target student.

Several factors are associated with the accurate and appropriate use of direct observation data collection methods. The use of short intervals (i.e., 5–10 seconds) over a minimum of 15 minutes per observation period has proven more accurate than simple global estimates of very basic classes of behavior such as out of seat, talking out, or general off-task behavior. The importance of simplicity in coding behaviors observed in direct observation has also been well established, particularly when high-rate behaviors are used to provide an index of on-task versus off-task rates. Coding must also be comprehensive enough to allow for discrimination of target students from the peer-reference group. In validating a classroom behavior observation code for students with externalizing behavior disorders, Butler (1990) identified one general measure (global on task) and five specific off-task behaviors (talking, out of seat, inactive, noncompliance, and playing with objects). School district normative tables and protocols for the measurement of on-task rates and other behaviors have been developed for elementary and secondary/middle school populations (Butler, 1990; Jewett, 1989). A typical application of the response discrepancy procedures and format is provided in Figure 1, which can easily be incorporated into a multifaceted functional behavior assessment for students with externalizing behavior disorders.

Technology-Supported Direct Observation

Increased access to new technology has generated a host of new data collection applications available to assist school psychologists and others collecting direct observation data on excess behaviors of students with externalizing behavior disorders in the classroom. The personal digital assistant (PDA), known under various proprietary names (i.e., Palm Pilot, etc.), offers a nonintrusive means of collecting direct observation data using response discrepancy, time sampling, or event-recording procedures. The Comprehensive Behavior Tracking System (Oswald, 2000) is a PDA software package that allows users to gather a variety of data on targeted excess behaviors and on-task/off-task behaviors on a single student or several students. In the response-discrepancy mode, the observer can make comparisons between a student and the whole class in terms of on-task percentages using 10, 20, 30 or 60-second intervals for up to 15 minutes. The user sets an audible signal for random or equal intervals and records behaviors occurring with each signal. Teacher interactions with the student are also recorded. Additionally, event or frequency recording may be used to track multiple behaviors on as many as seven students within a specified time block. The user simply enters abbreviations for behaviors that will be tracked and corresponding keys are pressed each time the student engages in a target behavior(s). Data summaries and files can be edited and saved to a memo pad within the PDA or transferred to commonly available spreadsheets or text files on a personal computer.

The combination of response-discrepancy procedures with the use of a personal digital assistant and the CBTS software improves the efficiency of direct observation data collection in the classroom or other educational environments. Thus, for students with externalizing behavior disorders, direct observation methods can more easily be incorporated into a multifaceted functional behavior assessment for a variety of low/high rate excess behaviors.

Behavior Observation Form

Target Student ______________________ M/F ___ Grade _____ Date ______________

School ______________________ Teacher ______________________

Observer ____

Class Activity ____

Position ❑ Teacher directed whole class ❑ Teacher directed small group ❑ Independent work session

DIRECTIONS: Ten-second interval. Observe each student once; then record data. This is a partial interval recording. If possible, collect full 15 minutes under teacher directed or independent condition. If not, put a slash when classroom condition changes. **Classmates observed must be the same sex as the target student.**

1 2 3

Target Student*

*Classmates of same sex.

4 5 6

Target Student*

*Classmates of same sex.

7 8 9

Target Student*

*Classmates of same sex.

10 11 12

Target Student*

*Classmates of same sex.

13 14 15

Target Student*

*Classmates of same sex.

NOTE: To observe class—begin with the first same sex student in row 1. Record each subsequent same sex student in following intervals. Data reflect an average of classroom behavior. **Skip unobservable students.**

ON-TASK CODES: Eye contact with teacher or task and performing the requested task.

OFF-TASK CODES:

T = **Talking Out/Noise:** Inappropriate verbalization or making sounds with object, mouth, or body.
O = **Out of Seat:** Student fully or partially out of assigned seat without teacher permission.
I = **Inactive:** Student not engaged with assigned task and passively waiting, sitting, etc.
N = **Noncompliance:** Breaking a classroom rule or not following teacher directions within 15 seconds.
P = **Playing With Object:** Manipulating objects without teacher permission.
\+ = **Positive Teacher Interaction:** One-on-one positive comment, smiling, touching, or gesture.
\- = **Negative Teacher Interaction:** One-on-one reprimend, implementing negative consequence, or negative gesture.

From: Rhode, G., Jenson, W. R., & Reavis, K. (1992). The Tough Kid Book: Practical classroom mangement strategies. Sopris West: Longmont, Colorado.

FIGURE 1. Response Discrepancy Observation Form.

The ABC Approach

Another basic method used to assess excess behaviors exhibited by students with externalizing behavior disorders is the antecedent-behavior-consequence (ABC) approach. This method involves the description of an observable behavior and the recording of events that immediately precede (i.e., the antecedent) and follow the behavior (i.e., the consequence). The ABC approach to functional behavior assessment was first described by Bijou (Bijou et al., 1968) as a means to more fully assess a target behavior by evaluating the context in which it occurs. The behavior is, therefore, documented at the same time antecedent events and consequences are recorded. The ABC approach is based on the assumption that contexts provide both the stimulus for producing a behavior and maintaining it over time. Although data from the ABC approach generate hypotheses about potential relationships between specific behaviors and environmental events, the hypotheses are neither proved nor disproved. Instead, hypotheses are later tested through experimental manipulations.

The ABC approach typically involves the direct observation of behaviors, antecedents, and consequences, but this can be time consuming, and in some cases, nonproductive. For example, direct observation of low-frequency behaviors, such as fire setting, cruelty toward animals, and sexual perpetration against siblings and peers, is often difficult, if at all possible. The fact that these behaviors often occur in nonpublic settings makes it even more challenging to gather data and ultimately, to design interventions. The ABC approach may still be used, however, using structured interviews with informants (e.g., teachers, caregivers, neighbors, and at times, peers) who have astutely observed the student in the natural environment to obtain data regarding the antecedents and consequences and even the behavior itself. The purpose of these interviews are essentially the same as direct observations of behavior, namely gathering data about what took place before the undesirable behavior occurred, and what took place afterward to better understand the function a particular behavior serves, and what interventions are likely to be most effective. Knowing, for example, that a student strikes the family dog after being humiliated by peers on the playground, or sets fire to a field after being demeaned by a teacher for poor work, provides critical information about possible ways to decrease a student's inappropriate behaviors.

An understanding of the consequences of excess behaviors also may be important in designing effective interventions. Consequences that maintain behaviors, like antecedents, are not always predictable and vary widely across individuals. However, the majority of relevant reinforcers tend to be social (McComas, Hoch, & Mace, 2000). For example, individuals who set fires to buildings are often reinforced by the notoriety they receive, however, other fire-setters engage in this behavior solely for the intrinsic reward of watching and listening to the fire burn (i.e., sensory stimulation). Understanding how the consequences maintain a particular behavior, such as fire-setting, leads to the development of more effective intervention strategies. For example, preventing the student who is reinforced by social attention from viewing news coverage of the fire, or reading newspaper articles describing its damage, might be an effective intervention, while restricting sensory feedback is likely to be more effective in reducing this behavior for the student who is reinforced by sensory stimulation.

Undoubtedly, many low-frequency excess behaviors are as serious as high frequency excess behaviors, and in some cases, may have more dire consequences. Gathering functional behavior assessment data, even after the fact, is critical. One efficient way to accomplish this is by using the ABC Assessment Worksheet (see Fig. 2) described by Meuller and Jenson (Mueller, Jenson, Reavis, & Andrews, in press). In addition to recording target behaviors, the worksheet prompts the recording of information concerning a variety of consequences (e.g., positive and negative reinforcers, and punishers), antecedents, and replacement behaviors (i.e., substitutes for inappropriate behav-

Student's Name: _____   Date: _____

Teacher's Name: _____   Setting: _____

A   Antecedent – Something Before The Behavior

Time   _____
People
Places   _____
Events
Other Behaviors   _____
Down Time
                                _____

B   Behavior – Specific, Observable, Objective

Excesses To Decrease   _____

Or   _____

Deficits To Increase   _____

                           _____

C   Consequence – Something That Follows The Behavior

                                _____
Punishment
Positive Reinforcers   _____
   Attention
   Tangibles   _____
   Sensory
Negative Reinforcers   _____
   Escape
   Avoid

R   Replacement Behavior_____

Comments: _____

_____

_____

Jenson & Mueller

FIGURE 2.   ABC Assessment Worksheet.

iors). As part of a multifaceted functional behavior assessment for students with externalizing behavior disorders, the ABC Assessment Worksheet also allows recording of behavioral deficits, which may be critical in determining appropriate interventions to implement to reduce behavioral excesses. Completing the form over time also provides an opportunity to see if a pattern of behavior emerges.

Compliance Probes

The focus on basic noncompliance with verbal instructions has been described as an early antecedent of more serious behavioral excesses often manifested by students with externalizing behavior disorders (Rhode et al., 1992). A multifaceted approach to functional behavior assessment for this population would necessarily include assessment of behaviors that occur early in the progression and escalate to more serious behaviors like aggression, destruction of property, etc. Assessing specific precursor behaviors, such as compliance/noncompliance, may best be accomplished through the adaptation and use of experimental behavior "probes." Compliance probes contain elements of both analog and in vivo data collection methodologies (Roberts, 2001). A list of standard, discrete instructions are systematically given to a target student by an adult authority figure based on common expectations and requirements of the setting. Compliance rates are calculated on the basis of percentage of directions or requests completed. The use of compliance probes or "tests" dates back to 1981 when they were proposed to evaluate components of parent training to improve childhood noncompliance (Roberts & Powers, 1988). The advantages include high reliability (97% agreement) and high internal consistency, generalization across settings and responses, and good sensitivity to intervention (Brumfield & Roberts, 1998). Compliance probes also have the added feature of returning virtually no "false positives" and are excellent in terms of test/re-test reliability. Research summarized by Jesse (1989) indicates that standardized compliance probes showing low rates of compliance at time 1 (60% or less) show similar low rates at time 2. Most recently, Roberts and others have begun to quantify normal levels of compliance for specific ages and genders (Brumfield & Roberts, 1998). The first Compliance Test was proposed in 1988 (Roberts & Powers, 1988) and has been used in several subsequent research and clinical applications (Jesse, 1989; Rhode et al., 1992). There has been increased empirical evidence that the measurement of compliance provides a strong addition to the diagnostic picture when complemented by behavior checklists or ABC analysis. The process is relatively easy to learn and use, is much more sensitive to the developmental process, and controls for individual differences across instructional styles. This allows the assessment to focus on the severity of excess behaviors and also to efficiently judge the impact of any intervention.

A sample compliance probe for use with students who have externalizing behavior disorders is provided in Figure 3 and can be utilized as part of a multifaceted functional behavior assessment for this population. Using compliance probes, the observer (e.g., school psychologist or classroom teacher) selects a minimum of 10 specific commands, which a teacher has a high probability of using within a specified activity/setting. Compliance or noncompliance with each command is recorded and a simple percentage is calculated reflecting the degree of compliance for that student in that setting with that individual. Specific setting or individual features can be isolated using a multiple-probe format across the day in each setting. Compliance probes can be used initially to establish a baseline rate for noncompliance prior to intervention. Conducting probes after an intervention is implemented provides an opportunity to periodically judge the impact of specific interventions based on hypotheses of environmental events that may produce or maintain noncompliance for that individual. Although compliance probes may be more time consuming than other forms of functional behavior assessment, the data obtained can provide a wealth of infor-

Teacher Compliance Probe

Directions: Adult gives a request, waits 10 seconds and marks "Yes" or "No" if the child started the requested behavior or did not. It is important 1) to not repeat the request, 2) not reward child for compliance, 3) act natural after the request and 4) wait a full 10 seconds before acting or repeating the request.

1. Please sit down	Yes	No
2. Line up at the door	Yes	No
3. Put your books away	Yes	No
4. Bring your assignment to my desk	Yes	No
5. Be quiet	Yes	No
6. Look at me	Yes	No
7. Come here	Yes	No
8. Get a paper and pencil out	Yes	No
9. Write your name on the paper	Yes	No
10.Get busy with your assignment	Yes	No
11. Walk	Yes	No
12. Look up front	Yes	No
13. Come inside the room	Yes	No
14.Sit down	Yes	No
15.Go to your desk	Yes	No
16. Put your books away	Yes	No
17. Give me the _____	Yes	No
18. Sit up	Yes	No
19 Go to _____	Yes	No
20. Pick up the _____	Yes	No
Sample Requests from Specific Setting (classroom, hallway, playground)		
21.	Yes	No
22.	Yes	No
23	Yes	No
24.	Yes	No
25.	Yes	No

A minimum of 10 different requests marked across one week are needed to use the following formula

Total marked Yes ____ / Yes____ + No ____ X 100 ' **Percent Compliance _____%**

FIGURE 3.   Sample Compliance Probe.

mation regarding the effectiveness of changing antecedent or consequent events for students with externalizing behavior disorders.

FUNCTIONAL BEHAVIOR ASSESSMENT OF BEHAVIORAL DEFICITS

In addition to exhibiting disruptive behaviors in the classroom, children and youth with externalizing behavior disorders frequently experience poor school achievement as well as accompanying academic skill deficits, which places them at increased risk for poor long-term outcomes (Hinshaw, 1992). Additionally, their levels of academic engaged time (i.e., amount of time spent working on or attending to academic assignments) may be significantly lower than those of other students, averaging 60% to 70% of total time in the classroom (Walker, Shinn, O'Neill, & Ramsey, 1987). The co-occurrence of externalizing behavior disorders and academic difficulties has been estimated to be 10% to over 50% (Frick et al., 1991). To improve the school performance and potentially the long-term prognosis of students with externalizing behavior disorders, an accurate assessment of a student's academic skills should be incorporated into a multifaceted functional behavior assessment.

Functional Assessment of Academic Skills

Analysis of the factors affecting a student's academic performance difficulties can facilitate decisions on whether specific intervention strategies are necessary as well as assist in the design and implementation of the most appropriate interventions for that student. Following the functional behavior assessment paradigm, academic skills assessment might include indirect methods (e.g., interviews and rating scales), direct methods (e.g., classroom observation, work samples), and experimental manipulations (e.g., probes of a student's specific academic skills). Each of these methods will be elaborated on further below.

Semistructured interviews of significant adults across relevant environmental contexts might include the teacher(s) of that student as well as the student's caregiver(s), thus providing needed information about their perceptions of the student's academic performance in the classroom and during homework assignments. Interviewing the student directly may also yield meaningful information regarding their own perceptions of their academic performance and possible factors contributing to any academic performance deficits. These interviews can provide information about ecological variables that may influence that student's academic performance (Shapiro & Ager, 1992).

Another indirect method of assessing academic skills utilizes a rating scale format. For example, the Academic Performance Rating Scale (APRS; DuPaul, Rapport, & Perriello, 1991) provides a brief measure of a student's academic competencies in a classroom setting. The APRS is a 19-item teacher rating scale for children in grades 1 through 6 that uses a 5-point Likert format and results in three subscores: academic success, academic productivity, and impulse control. It has been demonstrated to be a reliable measure of students' academic performance based on teacher perceptions and it is uniquely focused on academic competencies rather than deficits (DuPaul et al., 1991).

Observation of students' academic performance within the classroom is a more direct method of assessing academic skills as part of a multifaceted functional behavior assessment (Daly & Murdoch, 2000). Direct observation data is often considered critical due to the potential for informant bias with indirect assessment methods. Observing rates of on-task behavior or academic engagement in comparison to typical peers in the classroom can provide crucial information regarding variables that may be contributing to a student's academic skill deficits. For example, a student who exhibits disruptive behavior in the classroom may experience infrequent teacher-directed queries because of the increased likelihood of difficult behaviors in response to such demands. Shapiro and Ager (1992) advocate using direct observation as well as analysis of student work samples to help determine the degree to which ecological variables may be impacting academic performance. Calculation of the work completion and accuracy rates of a student with externalizing behavior disorders can also help determine whether that student's academic deficits might be best characterized as a performance deficit or a skill deficit (Rapport, DuPaul, Stoner, & Jones, 1986). Brief curriculum-based measurement probes can also be conducted to ascertain the degree of match between the student's instructional level within specified curriculum and the current instructional materials being used (Shapiro & Ager, 1992). By moving the student to lower or higher instructional materials, a better instructional match may be achieved.

A more laborious and time-intensive assessment method is to conduct experimental manipulations or probes of a student's academic performance to determine the effects of various teaching strategies. Daly, Witt, Martens, and Dool (1997) describe five variables potentially contributing to a student's academic difficulties that can be tested using brief, experimental manipulations to confirm (or unconfirm) hypotheses regarding how those specific factors may impact the student's academic performance. The five variables include: (a) lack of motivation, (b) minimal skill practice due to low academic engagement, (c) lack of accurate feedback and assistance, (d) lack of match with instructional activities, and (e) extreme difficulty. The authors advocate setting up brief probes to test the hypothesized contingencies using curriculum-based materials as outcome measures. These probes involve brief presentations of specific instructional strategies that are likely to result in measurable improvements in performance. The authors suggest that selection of specific probes should be made based on hypotheses generated through more indirect assessment methods such as interviews and rating scales as well as more direct methods, such as observation. However, Walberg (1992) conducted an extensive review of academic performance research and concluded that providing formative and summative feedback to students and providing incentives to improve slow performance or inaccuracies were the two factors resulting in the most pronounced effects, suggesting that these two probes be considered as possible hypotheses. Indirect, direct, and experimental manipulation (probes) forms of functional behavior assessment specifically applied to academic skills are critical components of a multifaceted functional behavior assessment for students with externalizing behavior disorders to develop effective intervention plans.

Functional Assessment of Social Skills

In addition to exhibiting behavioral excesses, research has demonstrated that children with externalizing behavior disorders often demonstrate distortions in their interpretation of the intent of others' behavior as well as difficulty evaluating and generating solutions to social problems (e.g., Dodge, 1980). As a result, many children with externalizing behavior disorders experience significant interpersonal relationship difficulties, particularly with peers; they are at considerable risk for social rejection by their peers (Coie, 1990), and they often are rated as having very poor social skills (Carlson, Lahey, & Neeper, 1984). Because of the elevated risk for social skills deficits and peer relationship difficulties among children and youth with externalizing behavior disorders, a comprehensive social skills assessment also is warranted as part of a multifaceted functional behavior assessment.

Social skills are discrete behaviors that are learned and considered necessary for functioning adaptively in a variety of social situations, as well as important for school success (Sheridan & Walker, 1999). Determination of possible social skills deficits and the variables maintaining these deficits is necessary to develop and implement effective intervention strategies for an individual student. Generally, a multimethod paradigm is advocated in the assessment of social skills, incorporating multiple sources of information across multiple settings (Hops, 1983; Sheridan, Hungelmann, & Maughan, 1999; Walker, Colvin, & Ramsey, 1995). Application of the functional behavior assessment paradigm is warranted in this context as well. Therefore, social skills assessment might include indirect methods (e.g., interviews, rating scales, sociometrics), direct methods (e.g., playground or lunchroom observation), and experimental manipulations (e.g., probes of a student's specific social skill repertoire). These assessment methods are more fully elaborated below.

The significant adults within the student's various social environments are prime candidates for structured interviews, including the caregiver(s) of that student and the student's teacher(s). These individuals usually provide a wealth of information regarding their perceptions of the student's social skills and peer relationships across a variety of social contexts. Interviewing the student directly is not considered advantageous due to the likelihood of distortions in the self-perceptions of students with externalizing behavior disorders.

An additional indirect method of assessing social skills is using informant-rating scales. The Social Skills Rating System (SSRS; Gresham & Elliott, 1990) is regarded as the most comprehensive norm-referenced measure of social skills currently available (Flanagan, Alfonso, Primavera, Povall, & Higgins, 1996). The SSRS has good psychometric properties and is easily and quickly administered (Bracken, Keith, & Walker, 1994; Demaray et al., 1995). The SSRS includes a teacher rating form, a parent rating form, and a self-report form for adolescents, allowing for multiple rater comparisons. Parent and teacher rankings and ratings of students are minimally intrusive, inexpensive, and time efficient. Although social skills rating scales can sample a wide range of potentially relevant skills, they do not assess the environmental conditions (antecedents, consequences, setting events) that may be functionally related to those behaviors. Further, rating scales are influenced heavily by the perceptions of others and, as such, should not be used in isolation.

Based on inclusion mandates in IDEA and other federal legislation, students with externalizing behavior disorders may be included with typical peers in regular classroom settings for part or all of the school day. It has been well documented that the social status of children with disabilities is lower than their nondisabled peers (Gresham, 1982). Sociometric ratings by peers offers a unique perspective on social skills assessment in that it may facilitate determining the level of social acceptance as well as social rejection experienced by students with externalizing behavior disorders. As another indirect assessment method, forced-choice sociometric procedures are advocated that include ratings of all children within a classroom as well as an indication as to whether the target child is known well enough by the rater to be rated (Frederickson & Furnham, 1998).

Direct assessment methods, such as behavioral observations of peer interactions, can also provide an index of social acceptance difficulties or isolation as well as negative social interactions. A relatively inexpensive and simple observation method is to use a stopwatch to record any time the student is engaged in negative social behavior or the time the student spends alone, which can easily be converted to a percent of observation time that either of these two behaviors occurred within a particular social context, such as recess or lunchtime. Recording these same behaviors as they occur for one or more of the student's peers allows for normative comparisons with typical peers. To plan effective interventions, it also is necessary to assess whether the child has a skill deficit (i.e., the child does not have the necessary social competence) or a performance deficit (i.e., the social skill is within the child's repertoire, but the skill is not performed consistently or in the appropriate context) (Gresham & Elliott, 1984). Staging analogue social situations involving another individual who responds in a directed manner, allows for direct observations that can help determine whether the student possesses a particular social skill, rather than wait for an opportunity to observe the skill in a naturalistic setting. This is especially critical for social skills that have a low rate of occurrence. For example, the target student can be placed in a situation in which a peer needs assistance, such as a staged injury on the playground. Direct observation of the target student's response in such analogue situations can lead to effective intervention strategies for specific social skill building.

Although more time intensive, experimental manipulation probes can aid in understanding environmental events that may be reinforcing specific social behaviors for students with externalizing behavior disorders. It may be helpful to first assess the features of the various social environments of a particular student, including the demands of those environments and their behavioral contingencies (Sheridan et al., 1999). Specifically testing hypotheses about the function of individual social behaviors through direct manipulation of setting events, antecedents and consequences, allows for a more accurate determination of the variables maintaining particular social behaviors and subsequently, more effective interventions can be planned and implemented. Some research has shown that children with externalizing behavior disorders exhibit social skill difficulties primarily within the following three domains: (a) joining ongoing peer group activities, (b) responding to teasing or provocation by peers, and (c) complying with teacher demands (Walker, Irvin, Noell, & Singer, 1992). By focusing functional analysis probes on these three social skill domains (as well as any other hypotheses generated from interviews, rating scales and observations), the increased time and effort required to conduct such in-depth analyses would likely result in more effective intervention strategies specifically targeted to the needs of that student. A multifaceted functional behavior assessment that incorporates indirect, direct, and experimental manipulation (probes) methods in the assessment of social skills of students with externalizing behavior disorders can facilitate the development of useful, effective intervention plans.

CONCLUSIONS

The authors cannot overstate the importance of a multifaceted approach to functional behavior assessment for students with externalizing behavior disorders due to the unique interrelationships of behavioral excesses, behavioral deficits, and controlling environmental variables to plan effective interventions. The unique characteristics of the school environment also place a premium on efficiency and simplicity in terms of assessment and intervention and the vast array of functional behavior assessment methods can make the task appear overwhelming to school psychologists and educators. The authors have provided an overview of functional behavior assessment methods that have been validated on populations of students with externalizing behavior disorders or show the most promise for applicability to this population. Best practice guidelines mandate that school psychologists give thorough attention to all validated measures currently available. Another major focus of this multifaceted approach provides a means of linking assessment information to efficacious educational interventions that can be implemented and monitored in educational settings.

A balanced variety of functional behavior assessment methods involving the direct observation and recording of behavior, indirect data collection and interpretation (ABC approach), and the use of probes to establish baseline rates and measure impacts of intervention have been described. Due to constraints often present in educational settings, time efficient and practical functional behavior assessment methods have much to offer. Technology-assisted data collection and analysis using computer-assisted functional behavior assessment interviews and direct observation of behavior using new applications of personal digital assistant (PDA) based software offer opportunities to improve efficiency and reduce time needed to conduct and formulate adequate functional behavior assessments. The importance of addressing deficit-driven behavior (i.e., academic skill/performance deficits and social skills deficiencies) in addition to behavioral excesses is also an essential aspect of a multifaceted functional behavior assessment for students with externalizing behavior disorders.

REFERENCES

Alessi, G. J. (1980). Behavioral observation for the school psychologist: Response-discrepancy model. School Psychology Review, 9, 31–45.

Barkley, R. A. (1998). Attention-deficit/hyperactivity disorder. In E. J. Mash & R. A. Barkley (Eds.), Treatment of child-hood disorders (2nd ed., pp. 55–110). New York: Guilford Press.

Bijou, S. W., Peterson, R. F., & Ault, M. H. (1968). A method to integrate descriptive and experimental field studies at the level of data and empirical concepts. Journal of Applied Behavior Analysis, 1, 175–191.

Bracken, B. A., Keith, L. K., & Walker, K. C. (1994). Assessment of preschool behavior and social-emotional functioning: A review of thirteen third-party instruments. Assessment in Rehabilitation and Exceptionality, 1, 331–346.

Broussard, C., & Northrup, J. (1997). The use of functional analysis to develop peer interventions for disruptive classroom behavior. School Psychology Quarterly, 12, 65–76.

Brumfield, B. D., & Roberts, M. W. (1998). A comparison of two measurements of child compliance with normal pre-school children. Journal of Clinical Child Psychology, 27, 109–116.

Butler, A.R. (1990). Validation of a classroom observation code for behavior disordered and learning disabled students. Unpublished master's thesis, University of Utah, Salt Lake City.

Carlson, C. L., Lahey, B. B., & Neeper, R. (1984). Peer assessment of the social behavior of accepted, rejected, and neglected children. Journal of Abnormal Child Psychology, 12, 187–198.

Coie, J. D. (1990). Toward a theory of peer rejection. In S. R. Asher & J. D. Coie (Eds.), Peer rejection in childhood (pp. 365–398). New York: Cambridge University Press.

Daly, E. J., III, & Murdoch, A. (2000). Direct observation in the assessment of academic skills problems. In E. S. Shapiro & T. R. Kratochwill (Eds.), Behavioral assessment in schools: Theory, research, and clinical foundations (2nd ed., pp. 46–77). New York: Guilford Press.

Daly, E. J., III, Witt, J. C., Martens, B. K., & Dool, E. J. (1997). A model for conducting a functional analysis of academic performance problems. School Psychology Review, 26, 554–574.

Demaray, M. K., Ruffalo, S. L., Carlson, J., Busse, R. T., Olson, A. E., McManus, S. M., & Leventhal, A. (1995). Social skills assessment: A comparative evaluation of six published rating scales. School Psychology Review, 24, 648–671

Dishion, T. J., Andrews, D. W., & Crosby, L. (1995). Antisocial boys and their friends in early adolescence: Relationship characteristics, quality, and interactional process. Child Development, 66, 139–151.

Dodge, K. A. (1980). Social cognition and children's aggressive behavior. Child Development, 51, 162–170.

Drasgow, E., Yell, M. L., Bradley, R., & Shriner, J. G. (1999). The IDEA amendments of 1997: A school-wide model for conducting functional behavioral assessments and developing behavior intervention plans. Education and Treatment of Children, 22, 244–266.

DuPaul, G. J., Rapport, M. D., & Perriello, L. M. (1991). Teacher ratings of academic skills: The development of the Academic Performance Rating Scale. School Psychology Review, 20, 284–300.

Durand, V. M., & Crimmins, D. B. (1988). Identifying the variables maintaining self-injurious behavior. Journal of Autism and Developmental Disorders, 18, 99–117.

Durand, V.M., & Crimmins, D.B. (1992). The Motivation Assessment Scale (MAS) administration guide. Topeka, KS: Monaco and Associates.

Ellingson, S. A., Miltenberger, R. G., & Long, E. S. (1999). A survey of the use of functional assessment procedures in agencies serving individuals with developmental disabilities. Behavioral Interventions, 14, 187–198.

Ellingson, S. A., Miltenberger, R. G., Stricker, J. M., Garlinghouse, M. A., Roberts, J., Galensky, T. L., & Rapp, J. T. (2000). Analysis and treatment of finger sucking. Journal of Applied Behavior Analysis, 33, 41–52.

Flanagan, D. P., Alfonso, V. C., Primavera, L. H., Povall, L., & Higgins, D. (1996). Convergent validity of the BASC and SSRS: Implications for social skills assessment. Psychology in the Schools, 33, 13–23.

Frederickson, N. L., & Furnham, A. F. (1998). Use of sociometric techniques to assess the social status of mainstreamed children with learning difficulties. Genetic, Social, and General Psychology Monographs, 124, 381–433.

Frick, P. J., Kamphaus, R. W., Lahey, B. B., Loeber, R., Christ, M. G., Hart, E., & Tannenbaum, L. E. (1991). Academic underachievement and the disruptive behavior disorders. Journal of Consulting and Clinical Psychology, 59, 289–294.

Gelfand, D. M., Jenson, W. R., & Drew, C. J. (1997) Understanding child behavior disorders (3rd ed.), Fort Worth, TX: Harcourt Brace.

Gresham, F. M. (1982). Misguided mainstreaming: The case for social skills training with handicapped children. Exceptional Children, 48, 422–433.

Gresham, F. M., & Elliott, S. (1990). The social skills rating system (SSRS). Circle Pines, MN: American Guidance.

Gresham, F. M., & Elliott, S. N. (1984). Assessment and classification of children's social skills: A review of methods and issues. School Psychology Review, 13, 292–301.

Hartmann, D. P., Roper, B. L., & Bradford, D. C. (1979). Some relationships between behavioral and traditional assessment. Journal of Behavioral Assessment, 1, 3–21.

Hartwig, L. M. (2000). Reliability, validity, and utility of the Functional Assessment Intervention Program (FAIP). Unpublished master's thesis, University of Utah, Salt Lake City.

Hinshaw, S. P. (1992). Externalizing behavior problems and academic underachievement in childhood and adolescence: Causal relationships and underlying mechanisms. Psychological Bulletin, 111, 127–155.

Hinshaw, S. P., & Anderson, C. A. (1996). Conduct and oppositional defiant disorders. In E. J. Mash & R. A. Barkley (Eds.), Child psychopathology (pp. 113–149). New York: Guilford Press.

Hops, H. (1983). Children's social competence and skill: Current research practices and future directions. Behavior Therapy, 14, 3–18.

Horner, R. H. (1994). Functional assessment: Contributions and future directions. Journal of Applied Behavior Analysis, 27, 401–404.

Iwata, B. A., Dorsey, M. F., Slifer, K. J., Bauman, K. E., & Richman, C. S. (1994). Toward a functional analysis of self-injury. Journal of Applied Behavior Analysis, 27, 197–209. (Reprinted from Analysis and Intervention in Developmental Disabilities, 2, 3–20, 1982).

Jesse, V. C. (1989). Compliance training and generalization effects using a compliance matrix and spinner system. Unpublished doctoral dissertation, University of Utah, Salt Lake City.

Jewett, M. (1989). Behavioral observation instruction manual. Unpublished manuscript, Granite School District, Salt Lake City, UT.

Jones, K. M., & Lungaro, C.J. (2000). Teacher acceptability of functional assessment-derived treatments. Journal of Educational and Psychological Consultation, 11, 323–332.

Lennox, D. B., & Miltenberger, R. G. (1989). Conducting a functional assessment of problem behavior in applied settings. Journal of the Association of Persons with Severe Handicaps, 14, 304–311.

Lochman, J. E., & Szczepanski, R. G. (1999). Externalizing conditions. In V. L. Schwean & D. H. Saklofse (Eds.), Handbook of psychosocial characteristics of exceptional children (pp. 219–246). New York: Plenum.

McComas, J. J., Hoch, H., & Mace, F. C. (2000). Functional analysis. In E. S. Shapiro & T. R. Kratochwill (Eds.), Conducting school-based assessments of child and adolescent behavior (pp. 78–120), New York: Guilford Press.

Meyer, K. A. (1999). Functional analysis and treatment of problem behavior exhibited by elementary school children. Journal of Applied Behavior Analysis, 32, 229–232.

Mueller, F., Jenson, W. R., Reavis, K., & Andrews, D. (in press). Functional assessment of behavior: Can be as easy as ABC. Beyond Behavior.

Nelson, R., Roberts, M. L. & Smith, D. J. (1998). Conducting functional behavioral assessments: A practical guide. Longmont, CO: Sopris West.

O'Neill, R. E., Horner, R. H., Albin, R. W., Storey, K., & Sprague, J. (1997). Functional assessment and program development for problem behaviors: A practical guide (2nd ed.). Pacific Grove, CA: Brooks/Cole.

Oswald, L. K. (2000). Comprehensive Behavior Tracking System [Computer software], Salt Lake City, UT: Designer Edge Software.

Patterson, G. R., Reid, J. B., & Dishion, T. J. (1992). Antisocial boys. Eugene, OR: Castalia.

Rapport, M. D., DuPaul, G. J., Stoner, G., & Jones, J. T. (1986). Comparing classroom and clinic measures of attention deficit disorder: Differential, idiosyncratic, and dose-response effects of methylphenidate. Journal of Consulting and Clinical Psychology, 54, 334–341.

Reavis, K., Jenson, W. R., Morgan, D., Likins, M., & Althouse, B. (1999). Functional Assessment and Intervention Program (FAIP). Longmont, CO: Sopris West.

Repp, A. C., & Karsh, K. G. (1994). Hypothesis-based interventions for tantrum behaviors of persons with developmental disabilities in school settings. Journal of Applied Behavior Analysis, 27, 21–31.

Rhode, G., Jenson, W. R., & Reavis, H. K. (1992). The tough kid book: Practical classroom management strategies. Longmont, CO: Sopris West.

Roberts, M. W. (2001). Clinic observations of structured parent–child interaction designed to evaluate externalizing disorders. Psychological Assessment, 13, 46–58.

Roberts, M. W., & Powers, S.W. (1988). The compliance test. Behavioral Assessment, 10, 375–398.

Shapiro, E. S., & Ager, C. (1992). Assessment of special education students in regular education programs: Linking assessment to instruction. Elementary School Journal, 92, 283–296.

Sheridan, S. M., Hungelmann, A., & Maughan, D. P. (1999). A contexualized framework for social skills assessment, intervention, and generalization. School Psychology Review, 28, 84–103.

Sheridan, S. M., & Walker, D. (1999). Social skills in context: Considerations for assessment, intervention, and generalization. In C. R. Reynolds & T. B. Gutkin (Eds.), The handbook of school psychology (3rd ed., pp. 686–708). New York: Wiley.

Sidman, M. (1960). Tactics of scientific research. New York: Basic Books.

Skinner, B. F. (1953). Science and human behavior. New York: Macmillan.

Walberg, H. J. (1992). The knowledge base for educational productivity. International Journal of Educational Reform, 1, 5–15.

Walker, H. M., Colvin, G., & Ramsey, E. (1995). Antisocial behavior in school: Strategies and best practices. Pacific Grove, CA: Brooks/Cole.

Walker, H. M., Irvin, L. K., Noell, J., & Singer, G. H. (1992). A construct score approach to the assessment of social competence: Rationale, technological considerations, and anticipated outcomes. Behavior Modification, 16, 448–474.

Walker, H. M., Shinn, M. R., O'Neill, R. E., & Ramsey, E. (1987). A longitudinal assessment of the development of antisocial behavior in boys: Rationale, methodology, and first-year results. Remedial and Special Education, 8(4), 7–16, 27.

Psychology in the Schools, Vol. 39(2), 2002
© 2002 Wiley Periodicals, Inc.

DOI: 10.1002/pits.10027

GOOD, BAD, OR IN-BETWEEN: HOW DOES THE DAILY BEHAVIOR REPORT CARD RATE?

SANDRA M. CHAFOULEAS

University of Connecticut

T. CHRIS RILEY-TILLMAN

Temple University

JAMES L. McDOUGAL

Syracuse City School District

Our purpose here was to define and review the daily behavior report card (DBRC) as a monitoring and/or intervention technique. We considered a measure of a DBRC to be if a specified behavior was rated at least daily, and that information was shared with someone other than the rater. In general, it has been suggested that DBRCs may be feasible, acceptable, effective in promoting a positive student, and a way to increase parent/teacher communication. In addition, DBRCs are highly adaptive in that they represent a broad array of both monitoring and intervention possibilities rather than having a single, scripted purpose. All of these characteristics make the DBRC appealing for use in applied settings. However, an extensive, methodologically sound literature base does not yet exist. Despite the appeal of using DBRCs, widespread endorsement cannot be made without caution. We conclude with implications for use in practice and highlight areas in need of further investigation. © 2002 Wiley Periodicals, Inc.

School psychologists are increasingly being urged and even required to engage in behavioral assessment and intervention procedures for students in the public school setting. In fact, the recent reauthorization of IDEA (P.L. 105–17) now requires functional assessment and behavior intervention procedures to be implemented in the disciplining of students with disabilities. Effective behavioral assessment and intervention procedures in applied settings require the use of empirically supported, yet feasible techniques. While traditionally direct observation procedures have been heavily relied on for these purposes, these techniques have not been widely accepted for general use in schools. Our purpose here is to define and review the daily behavior report card (DBRC) as a monitoring and/or intervention technique that, in some cases, may be more applicable than direct observation for use in school settings. For our purposes, a measure is considered a DBRC if a specified behavior is rated at least daily, and that information is shared with someone other than the rater. In general, it has been suggested that DBRCs may be feasible (e.g., Nolan, & Gadow, 1994; Pelham, 1993), acceptable (e.g., Turco & Elliott, 1986; Witt, Martens, & Elliot, 1984) and effective in promoting positive student behavior (e.g., Blechman, Schrader, & Taylor, 1981; Dougherty, & Dougherty, 1977). In this review we summarize the available literature on the DBRC, identify areas in need of further investigation, and discuss implications for its use in practice.

Defining the quality indicators of behavior assessment and intervention often stimulates discussion over the most salient characteristics of these methods. For example, direct observation may be considered the "gold standard" of assessment measures because the rating takes place at the time of actual occurrence, and thus is generally considered superior to results obtained by indirect measures. In their review of the literature, Flugum and Reschly (1994) found that a direct

---

The authors would like to thank Robin Dobson and Marie McGrath for their assistance in the preparation of the manuscript.

Correspondence to: Sandra M. Chafouleas at the University of Connecticut, Department of Educational Psychology, 249 Glenbrook Road, U-2064, Storrs, CT 06269-2064. E-mail: sandra.chafouleas@uconn.edu

measure of behavior consistently made the list of quality intervention indicators. However, the benefits of direct observation often come at great cost, particularly in applied settings. Does the information gained from direct observation outweigh the level of resources and skill necessary to conduct it? Particularly in applied settings, practical considerations (e.g., time, personnel, skill) should be taken into account.

In addition to matters of practicality when selecting assessment and intervention methodologies, acceptability and use must be considered. Although direct observation may be the "gold standard," its application in the field has not always been well received. For example, Flugum and Reschly (1994) examined quality indicators of interventions and positive student outcomes. Self-report data by both teachers and related services school personnel indicated that less than half used a direct measure, which was defined as a measure of the behavior in the natural environment prior to intervention implementation (i.e., direct baseline data). Additionally, although other indices (e.g., behavioral definition, measurable goals) were associated with positive student outcomes, the use of direct observation measures was not. Nolan & Gadow (1994) have suggested that adoption of direct observation techniques beyond research applications or a limited number of residential treatment facilities has not happened given the required time and training. That is, direct observation is considered less practical than other methods in applied settings.

In summary, given the problems identified with the use of direct observation in applied settings, acceptable alternatives must be sought. Daily behavior report cards may provide one alternative to direct observation that is not only more feasible and acceptable, but also effective. Although an extensive, methodologically sound literature base does not yet exist, DBRCs have been shown to produce change across behaviors and populations. In this article we will summarize the literature on DBRCs. First, we will provide a definition and examples of its use as a monitoring technique and/or as an intervention component. Next, we will review an evaluation of critical issues relating to DBRCs. We conclude with guidelines for use and potential future research directions.

OVERVIEW OF DAILY BEHAVIOR REPORT CARDS

Daily behavior report cards have been referred to under a number of different titles, including home notes (Blechman, Schrader & Taylor, 1981), home-based reinforcement (Bailey, Wolf, & Phillips, 1970), daily report cards (Dougherty & Dougherty, 1977), and home–school notes (Long & Edwards, 1994). Within the literature on DBRCs, a consistent description or definition has not evolved, and a variety of options exist when creating a daily rating card. While the lack of a common definition or title has not emerged, common characteristics across DBRCs can be identified. These characteristics include (a) specification of a behavior(s), (b) at least daily rating of the behavior(s) occurs, (c) sharing obtained information across individuals (e.g., parents, teachers, students), and (d) using the card to monitor the effects of an intervention and/or as a component of an intervention. This broad definition of DBRCs allows flexibility to design the card based on the individual needs of a situation. This flexible nature also allows for multiple criteria to be manipulated to match the demands of a situation. For example, DBRCs can vary according to the behavior to be rated (academic, behavioral; increase or decrease in target behavior), type of rating system (checklist, scale), rating frequency (daily, more than daily, weekly), rater (child, teacher), target of rating (individual, classwide), frequency with which information is shared with another person (daily, weekly), consequence utilized (positive, negative), and setting of delivery of the consequence (home, school, other). In Table 1 we present a summary of these criteria, along with possible options and an example of each. In addition, we outline suggested procedural steps to take when creating a DBRC in Table 2. Next, we present a review of literature to illustrate the use of DBRCs.

Table 1
Criteria To Be Considered and Various Options Available When Creating DBRCs

Category	Possible Options	Example
Desired change in behavior	Increase in behavior Decrease in behavior	Decrease frequency of Johnny's calling-out behavior during teacher instruction
Frequency of data collection	Daily Weekly	DBRC completed twice a day
Rater	Self Teacher Both self and teacher	Joint rating by Johnny and teacher
Rating system	Checklist Scale	☐ No call-outs ☐ 1–2 call-outs ☐ 2–3 call-outs ☐ 4+ callouts
Focus of rating	Individual Small-group Classwide	Johnny
Contingency used	Positive reinforcement Negative reinforcement Positive punishment Negative punishment	Praise and tangible reward
Setting of consequence delivery	Home School Other	Praise—home and school, Reward—home
Schedule of consequence delivery	Daily Weekly	Daily praise Weekly reward

One of few studies primarily focused on the investigation of DBRCs was conducted by Dougherty and Dougherty (1977). The participants in this study included a class of fourth grade students attending a private school whose teacher indicated that they exhibited mild behavioral problems, including low homework completion rates and talking-out during group instruction. A multiple baseline design across behaviors was implemented using percentage of entire class exhibiting the behavior as the dependent variable (whole class target). The daily report card used in this experiment included a definition of each target behavior (e.g., homework completion, homework accuracy, talk-outs) and a place to rate each behavior on a scale from 1 to 4 (rating scale, daily rating). Examination of the first target behavior, homework completion rate, over the course of the study indicated a decrease in the percentage of students not completing homework from 35% at baseline to around 17% at the completion of the study. The second target behavior, talk-outs, also exhibited a decrease, from 13.5 per hour at baseline to approximately 2.3 per hour at the end of the study. The decreases continued even after the report card was rated daily yet sent home only at the end of the week (daily then fade to weekly).

An interesting aspect of the study is that neither the teacher nor the parents were provided specific instructions on interaction (consequence or setting of consequence delivery not specified). For example, the teacher's comments to each student while completing the rating card was not

Table 2
Steps Toward Creating a Daily Behavior Report Card

1. Define the target behavior(s), preferably in both positive and specific terms.
2. Decide the rating frequency and type of scale.
3. Design the actual rating card, considering feedback from all involved.
   Hint: Make sure to indicate the behavior and goal on the card.
4. Define criteria for receiving consequences (positive and/or negative).
   Hint: Initial goals should be set so that child can be successful.
5. Generate a list of potential consequences.
   Hint: Make sure the consequences are not typically received to keep potency high.
6. Define each person's responsibilities.

Note. Adapted from Long and Edwards (1994).

controlled. Similarly, while parents were sent a letter that described the report card and made suggestions about reviewing it with the child, no follow-up was conducted. One advantage to this lack of specification is that positive results were obtained without significant interference in the natural environment by researchers, or significant cost to teachers (the program was conducted with less than 2 hours of consultation). Teachers and parents were free to interact with students as they would normally. However, given the lack of rigorous experimental control, it is difficult to determine which aspect(s) of the intervention contributed to the behavioral change. In addition, given the atypical sample characteristics (i.e., private school, minor behavioral problems), it is not possible to widely generalize findings.

Another early example of the use of a DBRC comes from Lahey, Gendrich, Gendrich, Schnelle, Gant and McNees (1977). These authors investigated behavior of kindergarten children during "rest period." In this study, teachers were asked to accurately complete a behavior report card for each student (individual student yet whole class included) at the end of each school day (once daily rating), and to provide feedback to the students in a positive manner (positive consequence). Each report contained a checklist of five positive statements along with a space to write something positive about the child's day (checklist format). The first daily report card sent to the parents was accompanied by a letter prompting them to tell their children they did a good job when a positive report was received, and to avoid punishing them for poor reports (positive consequence). Independent observers recorded the occurrence of distracting, resting, and sleeping behavior during rest time (mild behavior problem, increase in correct behavior desired). Over the course of the study, both an increase in the number of intervals in which students were appropriately resting and sleeping, and a decrease in the average percent of children exhibiting distracting behavior were observed. However, it should be noted that the strength of agreement between the teacher rating and the direct observation data was not reported. The authors contend that because teachers were able to provide effective feedback and assistance, the DBRCs was an efficient intervention technique.

A final example illustrating the use of DBRCs can be found in a study conducted by Blechman et al. (1981). This study emphasized a conjoint relationship between home and school in that the home served as the primary setting for delivery of a positive consequence. In this study, students in 17 elementary classrooms were randomly assigned to a home-note, family problem solving or, an untreated control condition. The focus of the intervention was to increase student consistency (reduced scatter compared to baseline performance) in math work completion. During the intervention for children in the home-note and family problem solving groups, the teachers scored children's math work and sent home a "good-news note" when the child received a score at or above his or her baseline mean. The primary differentiating factor between the two groups was the level of contact with the parents. For parents in the family problem solving condition, a 1-hour meeting was held before the start of the intervention in which the intervention was discussed and a contingency contract was specified. Throughout the intervention, weekly telephone contacts were made with parents to remind them of the instructions for delivering the reward. Parents in the home-note condition received a letter about the intervention, along with suggestions for delivering positive consequences. Upon receipt of a "good-news" note, parents in both intervention conditions provided a reward in the home. The results of this study indicated that both of the intervention groups produced greater consistency over the control condition as measured by a scatter index. However, while the control and home-note students decreased their math accuracy, the family problem solving maintained accuracy across reinforced and nonreinforced probes. In summary, it appeared that more frequent home and school contact and skill training regarding the intervention was most effective.

In summary, the DBRC does not refer to a single procedure, but a group of techniques possessing similar broad characteristics. These characteristics involve a specified behavior(s) that is rated at least daily, with the rating information then shared with persons in other setting(s). The DBRC may serve either to monitor the effects of an intervention and/or as a component of the intervention. Within these guidelines, a wide variety of options exist to tailor a DBRC to meet the needs of a situation. These options may be one of the most appealing aspects of DBRCs. Flexibility, along with additional reasons for the appeal of DBRCs, are discussed below.

WHY ARE DAILY BEHAVIOR REPORT CARDS APPEALING?

Daily behavior report cards are intuitively appealing to educators, as they can provide a simple, inexpensive, and flexible method of providing frequent feedback to students and parents. Dougherty and Dougherty (1977) identified flexibility (e.g., variation in scale complexity, ease of scale alteration) in providing feedback to students at regular intervals as a very positive feature of DBRCs. This flexible nature comes from the ability to easily individualize the card to create a simple procedure for daily ratings. For example, specificity of the behavior to be rated can range from broad descriptors (e.g., "good" to "poor") to precise definitions (e.g., no talk-outs" to "more than two talk-outs"). Another appealing aspect of DBRCs is that their use requires only minor changes in existing classroom practices (Lahey et al., 1977). Daily behavior report cards' completion time has been estimated between 10 seconds and slightly less than 1 minute per student. Additionally, in a review of factors involved in the evaluation of school performance of students with attention deficit hyperactivity disorder, Pelham (1993) advocated for a method that is ecologically valid, sensitive to individual differences in medication response, and feasible to implement (i.e., requiring minimal training). He recommended the use of daily report cards as they can meet these criteria in addition to serving as a dependent measure and as part of a behavioral intervention. Given these features, DBRCs seem well suited for use in applied settings.

The potential dual role for DBRCs to serve as both a monitoring device and an intervention component may be a primary reason for its appeal in applied settings. The use of DBRCs to assess (i.e., monitor) children's behavior provides data to inform intervention design and evaluation. A number of articles addressing the need for school feedback when determining appropriate pharmacotherapy protocols for children with Attention-Deficit Hyperactivity Disorder have incorporated the use of teacher ratings and/or DBRCs (See Nolan & Gadow, 1994; Pelham, 1993). In a case example, an individualized and operationalized daily report card demonstrated greater sensitivity to medication effects than did other measures (e.g., brief teacher ratings) (Pelham, 1993). The author concluded that DBRCs possessed utility as a dependent variable in school-based medication assessments. Alternatively, in a study by Lahey et al. (1977), the DBRC was used as a tool to facilitate home–school collaboration. In that study, independent direct observation data served as the dependent measure. The card was used as the intervention component to provide daily parent feedback, but unfortunately the data from the card was not presented or used as part of the evaluation.

In contrast, Schumaker, Hovell, and Sherman (1977) demonstrated the use of a DBRC as both a monitoring and an intervention component. In a series of three studies, junior high school students served as participants. The DBRC consisted of a number of behaviors related to classroom rules (e.g., on time, stay in seat) as well as academic performance (e.g., contributes to discussion, uses time to work on assignments). Parents delivered the consequences (praise, privileges), and were trained in the process prior to intervention implementation as well as provided with follow-up phone calls. The dependent measure was the percentage of the behavior exhibited as rated on the DBRC. Thus, the DBRC served both as a tool to monitor student behavior of as well as a component of the home–school intervention. Overall results suggested that a combination of parent praise and home privileges produced the most positive effects on student behavior.

Another related reason for the appeal of DBRCs relates to the conjoint orientation to intervention and data collection. Clearly, one of the simplest limitations of any school-based intervention is related to the restricted setting. While children are in school for a significant amount of time, they spend the majority of their time in other settings, particularly the home. The child's home offers an opportune setting to increase the number of potential contingencies and promote generalization of any school-based intervention. Thus, the power of the intervention may also be increased. McCain and Kelley (1993) suggested several additional potential advantages of interventions with home components over solely school-based interventions. These suggestions included increased potency of available consequences, increased opportunity for parent/teacher communication, and shared responsibility for interventions. Additionally, Budd, Leibowitz, Riner, Mindell, and Goldfarb (1981) suggested that a home component to behavioral interventions may relieve some of the burden on the teacher to be responsible for the entire treatment program, and also supported that delayed reinforcement may promote generalization of treatment effects. The study by McCain and Kelley (1993) involved preschool students who displayed moderately disruptive behaviors. The rating card system, completed based on subjects' morning activity, involved teacher rating of specified behaviors and positive feedback two times per day. Subjects were granted or denied home privileges based on the ratings. Data collected by independent observers indicated subjects' on-task behavior increased and disruptive behavior decreased. Results were consistent following removal and reinstatement of the intervention. However, as the researchers made no attempt to distinguish between the effects of school ratings and feedback and those of home privileges, it is not possible to ascertain the unique contributions of each. The study conducted by Budd et al. (1981) with preschool and kindergarten children also incorporated multiple behaviors and treatment variables. However, these authors determined that home privilege may have been an essential component of the treatment for most participants. Only one of the participants demonstrated improvement with school praise and stickers alone. Even then, that student's improvement was not as great as when the home privilege was added. The authors also noted that low frequency problems (i.e., off area) may have been adequately addressed without the home privilege, but it could not be determined because the duration of school praise and sticker condition was too short to assess long-term effects. In addition, the authors cautioned that the intervention program was not sufficient for all of the participants.

Despite the potential opportunity to foster a conjoint relationship, Long and Edwards (1994) caution that adding the home component may not negate the need for in-class management when students cannot handle a long reward delay. In addition, interventions with a home component may be contraindicated for families with significant problems, as familial dysfunction may lead to low treatment consistency. In addition, positive findings regarding the use of a home component may not generalize to all students and situations. For example, in Budd et al. (1981) study, two subjects did not have successful outcomes with the home-based treatment. Although the specific reasons for this were not clearly identified, the authors suggested that developmental level of the child, the level of disruptive behavior, and parental inconsistency may have been important factors.

In summary, it is obvious that DBRCs possess many appealing aspects (e.g., flexibility, dual purpose to monitor and as intervention, conduit to increase home–school communication), and have demonstrated efficacy in a variety of situations. However, comprehension evaluation with regard to other pertinent characteristics such as accuracy, reliability, and validity has not occurred. This type of evaluation is critical to develop complete understanding of the use and potential misuse of DBRCs.

EVALUATING DAILY BEHAVIOR REPORT CARDS

It is difficult to comprehensively and conclusively evaluate literature on DBRCs for two reasons: (1) the limited availability of such research, and (2) inconsistency in definitions/criteria used. Most researchers have investigated DBRCs as one aspect of a study, usually as a supplemental measure (see Forgatch & Ramsey, 1994; Nolan & Gadow, 1994). As discussed previously, some researchers have used DBRCs solely as an intervention tool rather than combined as a monitoring device. Although the simultaneous use of DBRCs to monitor and in the intervention could positively contribute to their treatment utility, the benefits are questionable if the assessment does not provide accurate, reliable, and valid data.

Each of the studies described thus far provides interesting information, but none entailed a comprehensive evaluation of daily report cards as a monitoring device, an intervention tool, or as both. For example, no study assessed the accuracy of teacher ratings on the cards. When evaluating the psychometric adequacy of a functional approach to behavioral assessment, Cone (1997) presents a number of considerations. Given the scarcity of available literature on DBRCs and the lack of specificity in defining the term, it is not possible to evaluate DBRCs on all of the suggested criteria. However, some of the concepts provide a valuable framework to use in evaluating existing literature on DBRCs. One criterion involves assessing the accuracy of the measure (i.e., representational validity). That is, how well does it assess what it is supposed to measure? Does it have sufficient sensitivity to detect the occurrence of the behavior? For a behavioral measure, one way to assess this is to determine if other measures produce similar information. Nolan and Gadow (1994) suggested the ecological validity of behavior rating scales could be determined using direct observation as the standard. A second issue relates to reliability, or the consistency of the measurement involved. In the case of DBRCs, it is important to examine whether the information gathered is dependent on the person providing the information, as well as the consistency of information over time. A third consideration relates to other aspects of validity including elaborative validity, or the utility or practical value of the measure (Cone, 1997). Examination of social validity may be one way to assess the practical value of DBRCs. That is, if the person intended to use the DBRC perceives it as acceptable, then the DBRC has practical value. We next examine DBRCs on each of these three criteria (i.e., accuracy, reliability, social validity).

Accuracy

The need for accuracy in the use of DBRCs is illustrated in a study conducted by Bailey et al. (1970) of five boys living in a residential home for pre-delinquent children. Teacher daily reports included checking "yes" or "no" regarding whether or not each student obeyed classroom rules and engaged in study behavior during math. Students receiving a "yes" mark in both areas were provided points toward the token economy system in the residential home. Teachers were not responsible for determining which check to make as observers recorded student behavior and indicated when the teacher should check "yes" (i.e., positive rating at least 90% of the time). The results produced significant decreases in misbehavior and increases in the amount and accuracy of work completed. However, these changes were not evidenced during a phase in which "yes" marks were provided noncontingent on actual behavior. Thus, findings suggest that effective use of DBRCs is contingent on accurate rating of student behavior. Further, given the use of observers as the monitors, no information was available regarding whether or not teachers could independently make accurate ratings of student behavior.

Additional studies that have used DBRCs as intervention tools also collected direct observation data as the dependent measure. Unfortunately, this information was not compared to the DBRC rating as way to assess rating accuracy (see Budd et al., 1981; McCain & Kelley, 1993). Related evidence of the correspondence with direct observation data can be found in literature investigating teacher feedback used in medication monitoring for students with Attention-Deficit Hyperactivity Disorder (Nolan & Gadow, 1994; Pelham, 1993). In these studies, the IOWA Conners Teacher Rating Scale (Loney & Milich, 1982; a brief scale assessing oppositional/defiant behaviors and inattention/overactivity behaviors) was utilized as the teacher-rating instrument. It was created based on identification of items from relevant factors of the Conners Teacher Rating Scale that demonstrated "significant and unique contributions in predicting observed classroom behaviors" (Pelham, Milich, Murphy & Murphy, 1989). Nolan and Gadow (1994) directly investigated the concurrent relation between brief teacher ratings and classroom observations as measures of children's responses to stimulant drugs. In their study, the brief teacher-completed ratings and percentage of behavioral occurrence using whole interval recording were correlated using data for each taken on the same day. [Note that the ratings consisted of the entire scale and thus were not individualized for each specific student (i.e., may have rated some behaviors that were not related to the student's behavior problems).] The results were presented in the form of group findings, thus, the authors note that the findings may not necessarily be representative for individual students. However, on the basis of the group findings, the authors contend that the scales provided reasonably good characterizations of more disruptive negative behaviors (e.g., disturbing peers, noncompliance with teacher, nonphysical aggression). Lower correlations were found for less external behaviors indicative of inattention and overactivity.

In contrast to these findings, Fuchs and Fuchs (1988) presented data from the Mainstream Assistance Team (MAT) project which suggested a lack of correspondence between teacher ratings of improvement and direct observation. In this evaluation, teacher rating across various forms of behavioral consultation indicated student gains in on-task behavior that were not captured by direct observation procedures. Greater gains on teacher ratings were associated with versions of behavioral consultation that included more consultation follow-up and support. However, interestingly, these student gains were not consistent with direct observation. When interpreting these findings, it is important to note that this data was summarized based on pre-post (2 pre, 2 post observations) rather than daily collection. To explains this conflicting data, Fuchs and Fuchs (1988) present two possible explanations that can be considered within the context of DBRCs. The first is that teacher ratings are inaccurate, and that teachers rated the behaviors as improved due to a desire to please the consultants. The second is that teachers are accurate raters, and may have perceived a change in student behavior that may not have been captured by the limited number of direct observations conducted. Implications of these explanations can be drawn in relation to DBRCs. That is, if a perception of change is enough to create a positive student environment, then maybe accuracy is not as important. For example, if the student was referred for a relatively minor behavioral problem, perhaps a positive teacher perception of the student would be enough to create a successful classroom climate for that student.

Reliability

Given the indirect (i.e., rating by other) nature of DBRCs, one important form of reliability to establish is inter-rater. In the first two of three studies on the use of DBRCs with junior high school students, Schumaker et al. (1977), conducted inter-rater reliability estimates at least one time in each condition (baseline, intervention). An experimenter attended each of the students' classes and independently completed a card. The two cards (teacher, experimenter) were compared on a point-by-point basis. Agreement estimates ranged from 78 to 90%. In the third study, school counselors were responsible for implementing the DBRC program. The two counselors were initially provided with a step-by-step implementation manual, which included directions to measure reliability. Only one of the two counselors conducted the reliability check. The authors noted that agreement for classroom rules was equal to or greater than 80%, and 100% agreement within one point for classwork performance.

Relatedly, Forgatch and Ramsey (1994) reported a study on the effects of an intervention to increase the quality of homework completion in junior high school students. Although the study included multiple treatment components (e.g., parental monitoring and rewards, teacher rating, informational materials on homework completion), one assessment measure involved daily rating of homework quality (i.e., Likert-scale) by teachers. When describing the results, the authors note that they were unable to use the teacher ratings as an outcome variable because individual differences in teacher perceptions were evident. That is, the three participating teachers rated perceptions of change in homework quality differently. A suggestion was made that ratings may be biased when teachers are included as participants in the intervention. Merrell (2000) provides an excellent review of error and bias in response that can be evident with indirect measures such as ratings by others. In general, cross informant agreement can be potentially low, particularly for internalizing versus externalizing problems or between self-report and informant report. In summary, although these results by no means are adequate to draw firm conclusions regarding the reliability of DBRCs, these results suggest potential problems with both agreement ratings and integrity of implementation.

Social Validity

Specific examination of the social validity of DBRCs is not available. However, implications of research in related areas may provide some insight into the potential validity of DBRCs. Social validity is an important consideration as its assessment attends to value within the context of the broader social environment (Eckert & Hintze, 2000). That is, with the use of DBRCs, the focus is not only on the child but also the teacher. One piece of social validity refers to acceptability (Witt, Martens & Elliot, 1984). Acceptability has been most commonly measured through subjective evaluation, or the incorporation of some rating scale to assess treatment effects by individuals working with the student. Eckert & Hintze (2000) summarized variables influencing the acceptability of treatments. One variable was severity of the problem. That is, interventions are rated as more acceptable when applied to severe rather than mild behavior problems. Acceptability ratings also are higher for positive rather than reductive intervention techniques. The implications of these findings may provide some clues as to why DBRCs appear to be used across settings and populations. For example, most DBRCs have been developed to include a positive consequence.

Although any form of acceptability research on DBRCs with adults is certainly limited, it is even more limited with students or children. Almost 20 years ago, Turco and Elliot (1986) stated that little is known about what students think about the interventions teacher use to change student behavior. Although no study has directly assessed children's acceptability of DBRCs, results of a few investigations may be related. For example, work by Turco and Elliot (1986) revealed that students prefer interventions that are home-based and positive as a way to change misbehavior. These results were consistent across age ranges and descriptions of problem severity. In an investigation of intervention acceptability with child psychiatric inpatients, Kazdin, French, and Sherick (1981) also found that children rated positive treatments as more acceptable. Taken together, these studies tentatively suggest that children would find an intervention with a positive home-based component, such as the DBRC, as very acceptable.

Only one of the studies reviewed reported parent acceptability through a general measure of satisfaction. Lahey et al. (1977) provided a follow-up survey approximately 7 weeks after completion of their study on the use of behavior report cards with kindergarten children during "rest period." The survey asked parents to respond using a Likert-type scale to questions about the daily report card such as its use as a way to improve communication, child's attitude about it, and use. The authors note that the items were biased in favor of positive statements. However, no negative comments were received from the 60% of parents who did respond. Overall, parents indicated support for the daily report card. Anecdotally, the authors noted that five other elementary teachers began using the daily report procedure after seeing it in use. Pulling together all of the findings in related areas of research, it can be tentatively suggested that DBRCs may be acceptable to children, parents, and teachers.

SUMMARY

Perhaps the most exciting element of DBRCs is that they represent a broad array of both monitoring and intervention possibilities rather than having a single, scripted purpose. Adaptability, along with the simple and inexpensive nature of the DBRCs, makes them an efficient and easy way to provide direct feedback about changes in student behavior. This increases potential involvement of and communication between teachers and parents. All of these characteristics appear to be important in applied settings. Despite the appeal of using DBRCs in an applied setting, widespread endorsement cannot be made without caution. First, the limited availability of research on DBRCs is problematic. For example, it is possible that DBRCs have good correspondence with direct observation, but it is not clear. Second, a number of concerns have been identified within the currently available literature. For example, as with many other school-based assessment and intervention techniques, Schumaker et al. (1977) suggested that the time required to implement a DBRC with integrity may still require significant resources. In closing, it is likely that the DBRC is currently being used without clear understanding of its potential for success, or which aspects of the DBRC should be included.

IMPLICATIONS FOR RESEARCH AND PRACTICE

Guidelines for Use

As discussed here, DBRCs refer to a category rather than a single entity. Although this offers great flexibility, some guidance is needed to select among the potential options. The flowchart presented in Figure 1 provides a model to help make decisions regarding the appropriateness of DBRC use. Obviously, the first decision to be made refers to defining the problem and deciding on the goals. Depending on desired specificity, identification of the problem may first include direct observation. Once these areas are specified, it is possible to determine if the DBRC offers a feasible method for addressing the problem. This can include consideration of resources available for implementation as well as how well the DBRC may address the problem or goals. For example, if a behavior has potential immediate harm to the child or others, a daily rating with positive praise is probably not initially sufficient to address the problem.

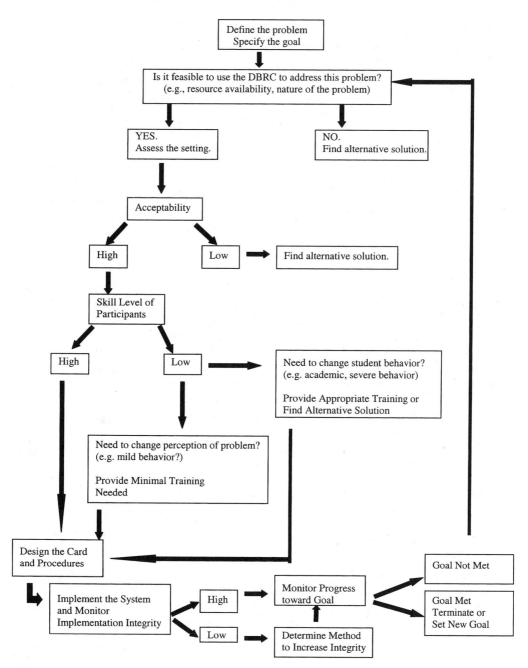

FIGURE 1.   A model to aid in decision-making regarding the use of daily behavior report cards.

If the DBRC appears reasonably feasible and appropriate, then assessment of the setting should occur. This entails examination of acceptability of the DBRC and skill level of the participants (i.e., teachers, parents) in using the DBRC. If the DBRC is not acceptable, than an alternative solution may need to be considered. If acceptability is generally high, then participant skill level can be assessed. If skill level is low, then reference should be made back to the identified problem and goals. If the goal is to change student behavior, such as in the case of an academic difficulty or a moderate-to-severe behavior problem, then it is necessary to provide skill training or else find an alternative solution. It would be unethical to implement an intervention for a more serious problem without providing sufficient skill in how the intervention is intended to work. In contrast, if the problem is minor, or does not pose major distraction or danger (e.g., pencil tapping), then it may not be as necessary to focus on accurately changing the behavior. In that case, it may not be necessary to provide extensive training in the DBRC.

Once acceptability and skill level have been ascertained, it is possible to design the card and procedures (see Tables 1 and 2). In addition, it may be helpful or necessary to consider the function (reason for) of the target behavior to maximize intervention fit. Finally, the DBRC can be implemented and progress monitored to determine if the goals are met. Progress monitoring may include use of the DBRC alone or in concert with a more direct measure, depending on the problem.

Implications for Future Research

Because daily behavior report cards are appealing for use in practice, systematic research is needed to determine the necessary conditions for effective use. Several areas warrant focused research attention. First, research could more closely examine various options when using a DBRC to determine if certain combinations are more effective than others. For example, the frequency with which information is shared between settings could be investigated. In other words, can weekly rather than daily reports suffice? In addition, are DBRCs more effective with particular problems (e.g., academic or behavioral, mild or severe)? Another possible examination of efficacy relates to the skill level necessary for effective implementation.

Second, research may focus on the role the DBRC serves in the functional assessment process. Support for the DBRC as a piece of an intervention is available, but its role in assessment is not clearly established. Can the DBRC aid in the accurate identification of a function? Related research suggests the DBRC may not be able to stand alone. For example, in an investigation of inter-informant agreement on the Motivation Assessment Scale (MAS; Durand & Crimmons, 1988, 1992) for a diverse sample of children with challenging behavior, low levels of overall agreement were determined (Thompson & Emerson, 1995). As a result, these authors contend that the use of indirect assessment approaches to identify behavioral functions should be considered as supplementary to direct observation or functional analysis. Only further investigation can reveal the role the DBRC can play in assessment.

Finally, investigation of current actual use of DBRCs in applied settings may be warranted. Answering questions such as the manner in which DBRCs are conceptualized and used, and their acceptability in actual school settings, may help to drive further empirical questions. Because the development of interventions that can be correctly and successfully implemented in the real world has been agreed to be of great concern (Rosenfield, 2000), the DBRC offers one opportunity to forge a stronger tie between research and practice given its potential feasibility. In summary, the DBRC offers both appeal and promise to both researchers and practitioners.

REFERENCES

Bailey, J., Wolf, M., & Phillips, E. (1970). Home-based reinforcement and the modification of predelinquents classroom behavior. Journal of Applied Behavior Analysis, 3, 223–233.

Blechman, E.A., Schrader, S.M., & Taylor, C.J. (1981). Family problem solving versus home notes as early intervention with high-risk children. Journal of Counseling and Clinical Psychology, 49, 919–926.

Budd, K.S., Leibowitz, J.M., Riner, L.S., Mindell, C., & Goldfarb, A.L. (1981). Home-based treatment of severe disruptive behaviors: A reinforcement package for preschool and kindergarten children. Behavior Modification, 5, 273–298.

Cone, J.D. (1997). Issues in functional analysis in behavioral assessment. Behaviour Research and Therapy, 35, 259–275.

Dougherty, E.H., & Dougherty, A. (1977). The daily report card: A simplified and flexible package for classroom behavior management. In L.A. Hersov, & M. Berger (Eds.), Aggression and anitsocial behavior in childhood and adolescence (pp. 73–93). London: Pergamon Press.

Durand, V.M., & Crimmons, D.B. (1992). The Motivation Assessment Scale. Topeka, KS: Monaco & Associates.

Eckert, T.L., & Hintze, J.M. (2000). Behavioral conceptions and applications of acceptability: Issues related to service delivery and research methodology. School Psychology Quarterly, 15, 123–148.

Flugum, K.R., & Reschly, D.J. (1994). Prereferral interventions: Quality indices and outcomes. Journal of School Psychology, 32, 1–14.

Forgatch, M.S., & Ramsey, E. (1994). Boosting homework: A video tape link between families and schools. School Psychology Review, 23, 472–484.

Fuchs, D., & Fuchs, L.S. (1987). Mainstream assistance teams to accommodate difficult to teach students in general education. In J.L. Graden, J.E. Zins, & M. E. Curtis (Eds.), Alternate educational delivery systems: Enhancing instructional options for all students. Bethesda, MD: National Association of School Psychologists.

Kazdin, A.E., French, N.H., & Sherick, R.B. (1981). Acceptability of alternative treatments for children: Evaluation of inpatient children, parents, and staff. Journal of Consulting and Clinical Psychology, 49, 900–907.

Lahey, B.B., Gendrich, J.G., Gendrich, S.I., Schnelle, J.F., Gant, D.S., & McNees, M.P. (1977). An evaluation of daily behavior report cards with minimal teacher and parent contacts as an efficient method of classroom intervention. Behavior Modification, 1, 381–394.

Loney, J., & Milich, R. (1982). Hyperactivity, inattention, and aggression in clinical practice. In M. Wolraich and D. Routh (Eds.), Advances in developmental and behavioral pediatrics, (pp. 113–147). Greenwich, CT: JAI.

Long, N., & Edwards, M. (1994). The use of a daily report card to address children's school behavior problems. Contemporary Education, 65, 152–155.

McCain, A.P., & Kelly, M.L. (1993). Managing the classroom behavior of an ADHD preschooler: The efficacy of a school-home note intervention. Child & Family Behavior Therapy, 15, 33–44.

Merrell, K.W. (2000). Informant reports: Theory and research in using child behavior rating scales in school settings. In E.S. Shapiro & T.R. Kratochwill (Eds.), Behavioral assessment in schools: Theory, research, and clinical foundations (2nd edition) (pp. 233–256). New York: Guilford.

Nolan, E.E., & Gadow, K.D. (1994) Relation between ratings and observations of stimulant drug response in hyperactive children. Journal of Clinical Child Psychology, 23, 78–90.

Pelham, W.E. (1993). Pharmacotherapy for children with attention deficit hyperactivity disorder. School Psychology Review, 22, 199–227.

Pelham, W.E., Milich, R., Murphy, D.A., & Murphy, H.A. (1989). Normative data on the IOWA Conners teacher rating scale. Journal of Clinical Child Psychology, 18, 259–262.

Rosenfield, S. (2000). Crafting usable knowledge. American Psychologist, 55, 1347–1355.

Schumaker, J.B., Hovell, M.F., & Sherman, J.A. (1977). An analysis of daily behavior report cards and parent-managed privileges in the improvement of adolescents' classroom performance. Journal of Applied Behavior Analysis, 10, 449–464.

Thompson, S., & Emerson, E. (1995). Inter-informant agreement on the Motivation Assessment Scale: Another failure to replicate. Mental Handicap Research, 8, 203–208.

Turco, T.L., & Elliott, S.N. (1986). Students' acceptability ratings of interventions for classroom misbehaviors: A study of well-behaving and misbehaving youth. Journal of Psychoeducational Assessment, 4, 281–289.

Witt, J.C., Martens, B.K., & Elliot, S.N. (1984). Factors affecting teachers' judgement of the acceptability of behavioral interventions: Time involvement, behavior problem severity, and type of intervention. Behavior Therapy, 15, 95–104.

Psychology in the Schools, Vol. 39(2), 2002
© 2002 Wiley Periodicals, Inc.

DOI: 10.1002/pits.10028

IMPLICATIONS OF BEHAVIORAL MOMENTUM AND ACADEMIC ACHIEVEMENT FOR STUDENTS WITH BEHAVIOR DISORDERS: THEORY, APPLICATION, AND PRACTICE

PHILLIP J. BELFIORE

Mercyhurst College

DAVID L. LEE, MARY CATHERINE SCHEELER, AND DANIELLE KLEIN

The Pennsylvania State University

In this article, we explore the disconnect between applied behavioral research and classroom-managed applied behavioral research. Much has been written about the gap between experimental (basic) and applied research, but for the practitioner in the field the true gap lies between tightly controlled, externally supported applied research and teacher-managed, in-house supported applied research. To this end, the purpose of this paper is twofold. First, a model continuum is presented to guide researchers through the stages of theory development, basic research, applied research, and applied action research. Second, the theory and application of behavioral momentum is used to illustrate how this continuum can function within an applied behavioral framework. The results of this study suggest that an intervention developed from the theory of behavioral momentum can be implemented within the context of a classroom and affect positive change in academic compliance among children identified for learning/behavioral support. © 2002 Wiley Periodicals, Inc.

Much attention has been given to the disconnect between basic and applied research in behavior analysis (Mace, 1994; Mace & Wacker, 1994; Michael, 1980). In fact, Mace (1994) systematically outlined interrelated strategies to close the gap between research carried out in the laboratory (experimental analysis of behavior) and research carried out in the field (applied behavioral analysis). The goal to remedy this disconnect is to translate interventions that have demonstrated effects in the laboratory into viable interventions for humans in applied research (Mace, 1994).

Of equal, and to the classroom teacher/practitioner of greater importance is the disconnect between applied research and "really" applied research. Too often, attempted replication of applied behavioral research to the classroom loses the experimental rigor reflected in the original applied work. Without this experimental rigor, findings in the classroom are noted as incidental, qualitative, or anecdotal, all lacking experimental control. These findings also do not provide viable information to support or refute the existing database from which the replication came. In essence, we in the classroom (a) sacrifice internal validity (experimental control) and ignore the theory-application link in an effort to (b) maximize external validity (generalization) and promote a cookbook approach to problem-solving. Common ground on the basic-applied continuum must be established.

In some circles, this "really" applied research has been identified as an action research model (e.g., Calhoun, 1993; Sardo-Brown, Welsch, & Bolton, 1995) or a research lead teacher (RLT) model (Logan & Stein, 2001). Action research, as defined by Sardo-Brown et al. (1995) is (a) predicated on a practical problem (a necessary component in applied behavior analysis), and (b) carried out by the classroom teacher(s) (not a necessary component of applied behavior analysis). Calhoun (1993) defines such action research as individual teacher research or collaborative action research.

From an applied behavioral position, two key elements seem to be missing from the action research and RLT literature. First, no mention of the need for understanding tactics of behavioral

Correspondence to: Phillip J. Belfiore, Mercyhurst College, Education Division, 501 E. 38th Street, Erie, PA 16546. E-mail: belfiore@mercyhurst.com

research is made (e.g., experimental control via single subject design). The omission of experimental control within an action research/RLT framework creates a database not worth dissemination. Without such experimental control, it becomes virtually impossible to determine with any certainty the relationship between intervention effectiveness, or lack thereof, and behavior change. At best, AB-designed action research could act as a pilot for more controlled, applied single-subject research. Second, action research makes no attempt to link methodologies to a basic–applied foundation. Teacher-identified concerns prompt teacher-gathered data (Calhoun, 1993), but the connection of practice to basic research or theory, a necessary component, does not occur. The omission of a basic research or theory base promotes a "flavor of the day" approach to intervention strategies, increasing the likelihood of intervention ineffectiveness and time mismanagement. For example, proving "playground time" as a reward for early assignment completion is only effective if we see an increase in future assignment completion when playground time is made available. To make the assumption that "playground" is a universal reward misses the theory behind the concept of positive reinforcement. We may continue to provide playground time, even when no improvement in assignment completion is observed.

From an action research/RLT position, applied research methodologies and procedures demonstrated in published applied behavioral journals cannot be logistically carried out in the context of a real day with only those personnel assigned to that classroom. Methodologies requiring out of classroom data collection, multiple observers, time-specific intervention components are difficult to implement in the context of day-to-day teaching. What is necessary is an applied behavioral, single-subject designed research paralleling Calhoun's (1993) description of classroom-based action research.

A model must emerge that is characterized by practitioner (a) delivered intervention in the context of the day-to-day operations of the classroom, (b) collected data within the structure of the class day, and (c) based decisions as to phase and condition changes to ensure experimental control. Taking those variables of *action research not consistently found in applied behavioral research* (e.g., intervention carried out by the classroom teacher/practitioner in the context of the natural setting), and those variables of *applied behavior analysis not consistently found in action research* (e.g., establishing experimental control, an overt link to the basic-applied research base) a new link emerges. This applied action research link provides the external validity necessary to extend the basic-applied research continuum, while maintaining the control necessary for behavior analysis (See Fig. 1).

Applied action research can further extend the external validity of the research line (A), or it can call to question some aspect of the research line, from theory, experimental, or applied that does not hold up (B), requiring re-investigation of previous stages. We present an example of this basic–applied behavioral action research continuum using the theory of behavioral momentum.

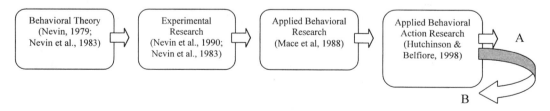

FIGURE 1.   Applied action model of behavioral research.

Behavioral Momentum

In 1983, Nevin, Mandell, and Atak proposed a theory of behavioral momentum in an effort to quantify the dynamics of behavior. Nevin (1996) theorized that operant behavior possesses a momentum that is analogous to physical momentum where rate of responding was analogous to velocity and resistance to change (i.e., persistence) was analogous to mass. In this analogy, behavior with a high level of momentum is likely to persist over time. In a series of basic studies Nevin and colleagues consistently found that baseline rates decreased comparatively less in the presence of the stimulus condition correlated with higher rates of reinforcement when challenged by extinction, noncontingent reinforcement (Nevin, 1979; Nevin, Tota, Torquato, & Shull, 1990), or an alternative reinforcement (Mace et al, 1990).

Applications of the basic research database on behavioral momentum have focused on increasing the rate (i.e., velocity) of a behavior within a given response class (Mace et al., 1988; Mace & Belfiore, 1990; Sanchez-Fort, Brady, & Davis, 1995). The application of the behavioral momentum model suggests that requests that have a high probability of compliance can be used to increase responding within the response class to such a level whereby compliance to low-probability requests is increased. The compliance and the subsequent reinforcement of the high-probability requests increase the amount of reinforcement for that response class, resulting in higher levels of overall compliance. Results from a series of applied studies showed that compliance to less preferred requests was enhanced when those less preferred (low probability of compliance) requests were preceded by compliance to a sequence of 2–3 highly preferred (high probability of compliance) requests or actions (Ardoin, Martens, & Wolfe, 1999; Mace et al., 1988; Mace & Belfiore, 1990; Sanchez-Fort, Brady, & Davis, 1995).

Additional applied research into behavioral momentum has begun to focus on academic behaviors in the context of the general classroom. Following a similar strategy as outlined by Mace et al. (1988) and Mace & Belfiore (1990), preferred, brief academic tasks have been shown to increase the rate of (Hutchinson & Belfiore, 1998) and decrease the latency to begin (Belfiore, Lee, Vargas, & Skinner, 1997) nonpreferred academic tasks in students with learning disabilities and behavior disorders. What made the work by Hutchinson and Belfiore (1998) and Belfiore et al. (1997) begin to address the category of applied action research was (a) the removal of specific teacher-delivered reinforcement, (b) the in-school method of data collection, and (c) the experimental control established using a single-subject design methodology.

The connect becomes more focused as we move from the theoretical and experimental work of Nevin and colleagues (1979; 1983; 1990), through the applied replications of Mace and colleagues (1988; 1990), to the generalized and applied action research of Belfiore and colleagues (1997; Hutchinson & Belfiore,1998). The purpose of the present study is to further illustrate the link between theory, application, and action. Prior works have demonstrated that delivering a series of 2–3 preferred mathematics problems decreases latency to initiate nonpreferred mathematics problems. However, the magnitude of the effects obtained was not large. The purpose of this study was to extend the applied work on behavioral momentum by attempting to increase the effects of the intervention in applied settings. More specifically, we examined the effects of quality of reinforcer on academic noncompliance by overlaying a negative reinforcement component to an existing high-probability sequence of mathematic problems.

Method

Subjects and Setting

Two students, Lance (age 10) and Megan (age 10) participated in the study. Lance was diagnosed with emotional disturbance (ED) and Megan was diagnosed with learning disability

(LD). Lance and Megan received total test standard scores of 93 and 82 on the Key Math (Connolly, 1998), respectively. The students attended an inner-city elementary school where they received special education services for learning/behavioral support in a self-contained classroom. The students were referred to the study for academic noncompliance (i.e., failure to initiate and complete academic tasks).

The instructional sessions took place in the student's regular classroom. This large room (approximately 10 m × 15 m) was subdivided using bookshelves so that two smaller groups of students could meet in the room at the same time or part of the room could be used for individual tutoring in the event that two groups were not meeting. Sessions were conducted on the side of the room that was empty using a one-on-one tutoring format common to many classrooms in this school. All sessions were conducted by a preservice practicum student who was working toward certification in special education.

Procedures

Preference assessment. The basis for interventions derived from the behavioral momentum paradigm is to use preferred requests to build a momentum of compliance that carries through to nonpreferred tasks. The first step in any investigation into behavioral momentum is to determine preferred (i.e., high-probability) and nonpreferred (i.e., low-probability) requests (tasks). We first conferred with the student's classroom teacher to determine possible preferred and nonpreferred tasks. The only constraint on task selection was that the students had demonstrated the skills required to perform the selected tasks, but typically failed to initiate or practice the tasks to attain fluency. The teacher suggested that multiple-digit and single-digit addition problems may serve as the nonpreferred and preferred tasks, respectively. Next, we used a forced choice procedure to empirically validate student preference for type of math problem. The procedures used to validate the high/low preference problems were similar to those used by Belfiore et al. (1997). Each participant was asked to choose and complete one of two worksheets. Lance's single-digit worksheets consisted of sixteen 1 × 1 digit addition problems and Megan's consisted of forty-five 1 × 1 digit addition problems. The multiple-digit sheets were comprised of either four 6 × 6 × 6 digit addition problems or five 9 × 9 digit addition problems for Lance and Megan, respectively. Problems were developed using a table of random numbers omitting the numerals 0, 1, and 2 to better control the difficulty level of the task. The number of digits required to complete each worksheet was equated for both worksheets so that worksheet preference would not be determined by fewer digits to complete, but would be a function of digit configuration.

During preference assessments, the preservice teacher placed one single-digit and one multiple-digit worksheet on a table in front of the student and asked the student to select one worksheet and complete all of the problems. The location (right or left) of the 1 × 1 digit worksheet was counterbalanced across trials. Three preference sessions were conducted each day for a period of 3 days (9 total trials). A 5-minute intertrial interval (ITI) was maintained between trials.

Baseline. Problem cards (21.5 cm × 5 cm), each containing one problem per card, were developed using information obtained from the preference assessment. The results of the preference assessment showed that when given a choice, both of the participants preferred the single-digit problems (high-probability) to the multiple-digit problems (low-probability). During baseline, each student was asked to complete a series of 10 low-probability problem cards. Students were given the following instructions; "Here is a stack of problems. Try to complete each problem as best you can and stack the finished problems here (preservice teacher pointed to an area on the table next to the student). Begin when you are ready."

Intervention.   After the baseline phase, two interventions were implemented. In the traditional high-probability condition (TRAD-HP), the students were given a stack 10 low-probability problem cards identical to those used during baseline, with the exception that each low-probability problem was preceded by a series of three high-probability problems. The instructions for the TRAD-HP condition were the same as those used during baseline.

In the escape from demand + high-probability condition (ESC-HP), students were given a stack of 10 problems similar to the traditional high-probability condition except that every other card had a dashed line through the problems. The instructions were the same as those used during baseline except that the students were asked to complete the problems on cards without the dashed line and to cross out and discard problems on cards with dashed lines. Because the participants did not have to solve the problems on the cards with the dashed line, the amount of work was half that of the TRAD-HP condition. Anecdotal information collected from the students' teacher suggested that math was aversive to the students as evidenced by noncompliance during class. By providing a way to escape demand we set up a situation whereby crossing out problems could act as a negative reinforcer. That is, the students could escape the aversiveness of the task more quickly by completing problems in a timely manner (i.e., the faster I complete this problem, the faster I can cross one out, and the faster I finish). Each student participated in approximately two sessions per week for 4 months.

Experimental Design, Measures, and Agreement

An alternating treatments design with reversal components was used to assess the effects of escape from demand and the traditional high-probability intervention on latency to initiate low-probability (nonpreferred) problems. For baseline, latency was defined as the time between the completion of one low-probability problem and the initiation of a subsequent low-probability problem. Latency during intervention was defined as the time between the completion of the last high-probability problem in a series and the initiation of the subsequent low-probability problem. To obtain a mean latency, the cumulative latency recorded per session was divided by the total number of latency opportunities.

Agreement data were collected throughout all phases of the study. During the preference assessment an independent observer monitored worksheet selection and procedures during 30% of sessions, with 100% agreement. For latency, an agreement was scored if the primary and secondary data collector's mean latencies for the session were within 1 second of each other. Agreement data were collected for baseline and intervention sessions for 24% and 10% of sessions for Lance and Megan, respectively, each yielding agreements of 100%. Treatment fidelity data were collected by the second independent observer during those same sessions using a checklist of the procedures. Treatment integrity was also 100%.

RESULTS

The results of the preference assessment showed that both of the participants selected the single-digit worksheet more often than the multiple-digit worksheet (Megan 9/9 trials and Lance 7/9 trials). Figure 2 shows the mean latencies for both participants. During the first baseline phase the mean latency between low-probability problems was 6.9 (range = 5.4–8.8) for Lance and 8.7 (range = 5.3–12) for Megan. The institution of the TRAD-HP and ESC-HP interventions resulted in a reduction of latency for both Lance (TRAD-HP *M* = 5.5, *range* = 4.5–6.8; ESC-HP *M* = 5.15, *range* = 3.4–7.4) and Megan (TRAD-HP *M* = 5.92, *range* = 3.7–7.8; ESC-HP *M* = 6.76, *range* = 4–8.4). During the second baseline phase the latencies increased relative to the intervention condition for Lance (*M* = 8.1, *range* = 7.8 ndash;8.4) and Megan (*M* = 6.2, *range* = 5.8–6.5). When the interventions were reinstated, the latencies once again decreased for both participants (Lance

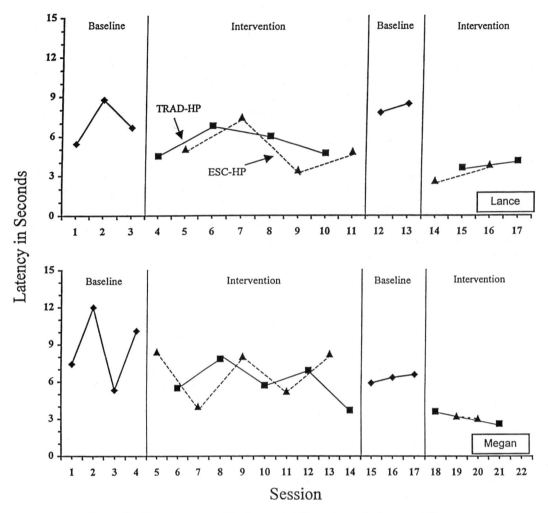

FIGURE 2.   Mean latency to initiate low-probability problems for Lance and Megan.

TRAD-HP M = 3.85, *range* = 3.6–4.1; ESC-HP M = 2.9, *range* = 2.6–3.1; Megan TRAD-HP M = 3.15, *range* = 2.7–3.6; ESC-HP M = 2.19, *range* = 2.6–3.2).

Overall, the TRAD-HP intervention decreased the mean latency to initiate the next problem in a given series by 37% for Lance and 41% for Megan relative to baseline. The ESC-HP intervention decreased latencies by 46% and 39% for Lance and Megan, respectively. However, only sight differences were found between the TRAD-HP and ESC-HP conditions.

DISCUSSION

The results obtained in this study contribute to the growing evidence on the effects of adding a series of three brief highly preferred academic tasks immediately prior to a nonpreferred academic task. Our results are congruent with those reported elsewhere that have demonstrated that high-probability sequences can reduce latency to initiate tasks and increase the rate of task completion—factors that can increase the number of learning trials that an individual can perform within a set period of time (e.g., a class or lesson) (e.g., Belfiore et al., 1997; Hutchinson & Belfiore, 1998). This increased learning time may aid in the attainment of fluency of skills for students who fail to persist at academic tasks.

Mace and colleagues (1988) have suggested that the addition of several preferred (i.e., high-probability) tasks or requests prior to a less-preferred request (i.e., low-probability) increases the density of reinforcement maintaining a given response class and results in increased compliance within that class. In addition to the density of reinforcement, quality of reinforcer delivered during the high-probability sequence may also affect compliance. Recently, Mace, Mauro, Boyajian, and Eckert (1997) found that when the quality of reinforcer within a high-probability sequence was enhanced, compliance to low-probability requests increased relative to lower quality reinforcers. Similarly, Belfiore et al. (1997) hypothesized that the reinforcers responsible for maintaining the high/low-probability sequence are highly individualized and could be positive reinforcement (i.e., one more problem or task completed) or negative reinforcement (i.e., one less problem or task to complete). For individuals with a history of noncompliance during math, providing escape from aversive math tasks may be a higher quality reinforcer than mathematics problem completion. For this reason, in this study a negative reinforcement component was added to the existing high-probability sequence to further examine the effects of quality of reinforcer on academic compliance.

In the current study no differences were observed between the traditional high-probability and escape from demand + high-probability conditions. Our initial hypothesis was that discarding problem cards could act as a negative reinforcer because the participants were able to escape the aversiveness of the task more quickly by completing problems. There are several possible reasons why there was no differentiation between conditions. First, the quality of reinforcement may not have differed enough between conditions. That is, the problems utilized in the study were not aversive enough to set up the negative reinforcement situation. Second, the latency measure was comprised of three operations: (a) reading the new problem, (b) computing the first part of the algorithm, and (c) writing the answer. The students may have been physically unable to perform these operations any faster regardless of condition (i.e., floor effect). Finally, the addition of the three preferred problems (high-probability) may have changed the valence of the task—making the task less aversive. This point may be particularly important for students who find academic tasks aversive (e.g., math). We did not have to reduce task requirements (i.e., compromise the curriculum requirements) to change the valence of the task to increase compliance. In fact, problems were added, not removed, to the task to change the valence.

A second goal of this study was to conduct research that met the criteria outlined earlier for applied behavioral action research. Specifically, the research had to be predicated on a practical problem, linked to a theory, be able to be carried out by classroom staff, utilize objective methods of data collection, and have some level of experimental control. First, this investigation of the effects of adding highly preferred single-digit mathematics problems on the latency to initiate less-preferred mathematics problems seems to meet those criteria. The students were both referred to the study because of a failure to initiate and persist at mathematics tasks. Ultimately, this failure to practice learned skills may adversely affect fluency and result in the students falling further behind in math. Second, the intervention examined in this study was based on the theory of behavioral momentum—a theory developed through extensive basic and applied research. Third, the study was carried out by a preservice practicum student within the context of the student's regular classroom using objective data techniques applicable to any classroom. Fourth, the data collected can contribute to the literature on academic and behavioral interventions because the experimental design allows for definitive statements to be made as to the effectiveness of the intervention.

The limitations of this study are related to the relatively small sample of students. However, these results replicate those obtained elsewhere. In addition, the response of both students during the second baseline in the modified reversal design did not completely return to the levels shown in the first baseline, suggesting that the students improved at the task over time. This improvement may have changed the valence of the nonpreferred low-probability problems. That is, the increased fluency may have made the low-probability problems less aversive during the second baseline, resulting in lower latencies than those demonstrated during the first baseline phase. However, the level of change observed when the intervention was reinstated for the second time suggests that practice effects probability changes in valence cannot account for all of the changes in latency over time. Finally, because we did not quantitatively assess the negative reinforcer used in this study, future researchers should develop methods to further assess reinforcer quality and its effects on behavioral momentum in academic settings.

IMPLICATIONS

Academic noncompliance (i.e., failure to initiate or persist at assigned tasks) can be a problem for classroom teachers as well as the students they serve (Hutchinson & Belfiore, 1998). Students who engage in noncompliant behavior are more likely to have difficulties in academic areas such as reading and mathematics (Adams, Snowling, Hennessy, & Kind, 1999). Typical approaches used to address noncompliance have generally focused on delivering consequences contingent upon compliant or noncompliant behavior. Ultimately, consequence-based methods rely on teachers to observe students and deliver consequences. This type of management system can be inefficient and difficult to implement on a classwide basis because teachers may fail to reinforce important occurrences of appropriate behavior or inadvertently reinforce inappropriate behavior. The research reported here on the use of behavioral momentum to increase compliance provides teachers with an alternative to traditional consequence-based methods of management. Interventions derived from the momentum model can be woven into the fabric of ongoing instruction as a proactive measure to increase compliance. After the materials have been developed, the intervention becomes somewhat student-centered, allowing teachers more time for direct instruction, which is key to academic success.

REFERENCES

Adams, J. W., Snowling, M. J., Hennessy, S. M., & Kind, P. (1999). Problems of behaviour, reading and arithmetic: Assessments of comorbidity using the Strengths and Difficulties Questionnaire. *British Journal of Educational Psychology*, 69, 571–585.

Ardoin, S. P., Martens, B. K., & Wolfe, L. A. (1999). Using high-probability instruction sequences with fading to increase student compliance during transition. *Journal of Applied Behavior Analysis*, 32, 339–351.

Belfiore, P. J., Lee, D. L., Vargas, A. U., & Skinner, C. H. (1997). Effects of high-preference single-digit mathematics problem completion on multiple-digit mathematics performance. *Journal of Applied Behavior Analysis*, 30, 227–330.

Calhoun, E. F. (1993). Action research: Three approaches. *Educational Leadership*, 50(9), 62–65.

Connolly, A.J. (1998). KeyMath revised: A diagnostic inventory of essential mathematics 1998 normative data. Circle Pines, MN: AGS

Hutchinson, J. M., & Belfiore, P. J. (1998). Adding a sequence of high-preference mathematics problems to increase low-preference mathematics problems performance. *Proven Practices*, 1, 12–16.

Logan, K. R., & Stein, S. S., (2001). The research lead teacher model. *Teaching Exceptional Children*, 33, 10–15.

Mace, F. C. (1994). Basic research needed for stimulating the development of behavioral technologies. *Journal of the Experimental Analysis of Behavior*, 61, 529–550.

Mace, F. C., & Belfiore, P. J. (1990). Behavioral momentum and the treatment of escape-motivated stereotypy. *Journal of Applied Behavior Analysis*, 23, 507–514.

Mace, F. C., Hoch, M. L., Lalli, J. S., West, B. J., Belfiore, P., Pinter, E., & Brown, D. K. (1988). Behavioral momentum in the treatment of noncompliance. Journal of Applied Behavior Analysis, 21, 123–141.

Mace, F.C., Lalli, J.S., Shea, M.C., Lalli, E.P., West, B.J., Roberts, M., & Nevin, J.A. (1990). The momentum of human behavior in a natural setting. Journal of the Experimental Analysis of Behavior, 54, 163–172.

Mace, F. C., Mauro, B. C., Boyajian, A. E., & Eckert, T. L. (1997). Effects of reinforcer quality on behavioral momentum: Coordinated applied and basic research. Journal of Applied Behavior Analysis, 30, 1–20.

Mace, F. C., & Wacker, D. P. (1994). Towards greater integration of basic and applied behavioral research: An Introduction. Journal of Applied Behavior Analysis, 27, 569–574.

Michael, J. L. (1980). Flight from behavior analysis. The Behavior Analyst, 3, 1–24.

Nevin, J. A. (1979). Reinforcement schedules and response strength. In M.D. Zeiler & P. Harzem (Eds.), Advances in analysis of behavior: Vol.1, Reinforcement and the organization of behavior (pp. 117–158). Chichester, England: Wiley.

Nevin, J. A., (1996). The momentum of compliance. Journal of Applied Behavior Analysis, 29, 535–547.

Nevin, J. A., Mandell, C., & Atak, J. (1983). The analysis of behavioral momentum. Journal of the Experimental Analysis of Behavior, 39, 49–59.

Nevin, J. A., Tota, M. E., Torquato, R. D., & Shull, R. L. (1990). Alternative reinforcement increases resistance to change: Pavlovian or operant contingencies? Journal of the Experimental Analysis of Behavior, 53, 359–380.

Sanchez-Fort, M., Brady, M. P., & Davis, C. A. (1995). Using high-probability requests to increase low-probability communication behavior in young children with severe disabilities. Education and Training in Mental Retardation and Developmental Disabilities, 30, 151–165.

Sardo-Brown, D., Welsch, L., & Bolton, D. L. (1995). Practical strategies for facilitating classroom teachers' involvement in action research. Education, 115, 553–559.

Psychology in the Schools, Vol. 39(2), 2002
© 2002 Wiley Periodicals, Inc.

DOI: 10.1002/pits.10029

REDUCING PROBLEM BEHAVIORS ON THE PLAYGROUND: AN INVESTIGATION OF THE APPLICATION OF SCHOOLWIDE POSITIVE BEHAVIOR SUPPORTS

TIMOTHY J. LEWIS, LISA J. POWERS, MICHELE J. KELK, AND LORI L. NEWCOMER

University of Missouri–Columbia

In an effort to reduce problem behavior, it is recommended that schools develop a continuum of positive behavior support (PBS) that focuses on prevention/early intervention as well as individualized student support systems for those students who display chronic problem behaviors. While there is a large database to support the use of PBS practices at the individual student level, the knowledge base supporting prevention/early intervention strategies is characterized as emerging. The purpose of this study was to investigate the efficacy of PBS prevention/early intervention strategies on the rate of problem behavior displayed by elementary school students during recess. Specifically, this study examined the effects of directly teaching playground-related behaviors and the use of a group contingency to reinforce mastery in an elementary school. Results indicated that the intervention reduced the frequency of problem behavior across three recess periods. Results are discussed with respect to support of an emerging empirical database and implications for practice. © 2002 Wiley Periodicals, Inc.

Schools confront a myriad of problems in their efforts to educate children and youth. One of the greatest challenges is managing student behavior. With respect to extreme management issues such as school violence, a recent report indicated that 1 in 10 American schools had at least one serious violent crime in the previous school year; 57% reported that one or more incidents of violence resulted in police involvement (U.S. Department of Education, 1998). In response to educators' needs for effective proactive management strategies, the U.S. Department of Education along with the Departments of Justice and Health have issued several reports delineating preferred and promising practices for students with and without disabilities (e.g., Dwyer & Osher, 2000; Dwyer, Osher, & Warger, 1998; U.S. Department of Education, 2000; U.S. Public Health Service, 2000).

One common theme that cuts across all the recent reports developed by education, justice, and mental health is the need for proactive universal prevention/early intervention strategies. A central focus found within prevention/early intervention is an emphasis on building prosocial skills, not simply reducing problem behavior. A second theme contained within current recommendations is to build a continuum of supports from common universal strategies to highly individualized behavior support plans (Sugai et al., 2000). Collectively, these two themes make up *positive behavior support* (PBS). Essential features of universal strategies of PBS include clearly defined expected behaviors, strategies to teach expected behavior, strategies to encourage and practice appropriate behavior, and consistency within and across school systems (Sugai et al., 2000). Building on the foundation of universal strategies, the next layer of PBS focuses on students who are "at risk" and offers targeted support for individuals and small groups of students. The third layer of PBS focuses on individual students who continue to display problem behavior. Key components of the "individual student" focus are thorough functional behavior assessments, instruction-based plans, and collaborative comprehensive plans that involve families and community agencies.

This research was supported in part by a grant from the Office of Special Education Programs, with additional funding from the Safe and Drug Free Schools Program, U.S. Department of Education (No. H326S980003), and a grant from the Office of Special Education Programs, U.S. Department of Education (No. H324T000021). Opinions herein are those of the authors and do not necessarily reflect the position or policy of the U.S. Department of Education, and such endorsement should not be inferred.

Correspondence to: Timothy J. Lewis, PhD, 303 Townsend Hall, University of Missouri-Columbia, Columbia, MO 65211. E-mail: lewistj@missouri.edu

While current recommendations to build schoolwide PBS plans that follow a continuum of service are firmly grounded and corroborated by empirical evidence supporting individual components, to date, there has been limited research evaluating the overall impact of the collective recommendations. However, several studies are beginning to emerge in the literature supporting the implementation of schoolwide systems of PBS. For example, over a 1-year period, Taylor-Greene et al. (1997) demonstrated a 42% reduction in behavior offenses that resulted in a discipline report by clearly defining schoolwide expectations and teaching students how to meet each expectation. More importantly, Taylor-Greene and her school team continue to show declines in behavior problems to date (Taylor-Greene & Kartub, 2000). Likewise, Nakasato (2000) demonstrated drops in daily office referrals across six elementary schools through the development of universal PBS strategies. Scott (2001) demonstrated 65% to 75% reductions in out-of-school suspensions and in-school detentions, which subsequently allowed students to be more successful in class to the point of increased standardized test scores.

A related recommended universal strategy is to build systems of support in specific nonclassroom settings such as the cafeteria, hallway, and playground. At this level, in addition to teaching positive expectations, routines and supervision are also deemed essential. For example, Kartub, Taylor-Greene, March, and Horner (2000) extended a middle school system of PBS to the hallway and demonstrated reductions in transition-related problem behaviors through a simple feedback system to the students. Lewis, Sugai, and Colvin (1998), through a combination of social skill instruction, active supervision, and group contingencies, demonstrated reductions in problem behaviors across the cafeteria, playground, and hallway within an elementary school. Colvin, Sugai, Good, and Lee (1997) demonstrated that through simple routine restructuring consisting of increased adult supervision, problem behaviors during the start of the school day were significantly reduced.

One setting that is noted as especially problematic at the elementary level is the playground (Colvin & Lowe, 1986). During recess, schools typically combine large groups of students in a setting with low structures and minimal adult supervision, a combination that often contributes to problem behavior and issues of safety (Hendricks, 1993). Thompson (1991) reported that more than 170,000 children are injured each year on playgrounds in America. In response to recess concerns, Lewis, Colvin, and Sugai (2000) demonstrated that increases in adult active supervision significantly reduced the rate of problem behavior observed during recess.

All of the studies to date focusing on the development of universal strategies of PBS are encouraging and are providing empirical evidence to support the combination of individual strategies into comprehensive schoolwide packages. However, additional data are clearly needed. In particular, replications of the studies described previously, in addition to others, must occur across a variety of schools with diverse demographics to create a broader knowledge base. To this end, the purpose of this study was to evaluate the effectiveness of an applied universal PBS intervention consisting of social skill instruction and group contingencies on the frequency of problem behavior displayed by elementary students on the playground. Specifically, we were interested in the efficacy of universal PBS strategies within a school that is characterized as at risk due to large percentages of students coming from impoverished and diverse environments combined with a large annual turnover in the student body.

METHOD

Participants and Setting

All students, grades kindergarten through sixth, participated in this study. The suburban elementary school served approximately 450 students, of which 70% were African Americans, 28% Whites, and 2% other; 47% of the total school population received free or reduced lunch. An additional challenge in this school was a large turnover in student population: approximately 50% over the school year. Turnover was largely due to the overall transient nature of the population this elementary school served.

The targeted setting for this study was the playground, which consisted of an upper and lower play area. The upper playground included a blacktop play area (basketball courts, four square, and designated area for jump rope), two tether ball centers, one swing set, jungle gym, and a kickball field. The lower playground included another blacktop play area (basketball court, designated jump rope area), one tetherball center, an activity center (slides, climbing tubes, platforms, monkey bars, and swinging rings), and a soccer field.

Recess was divided into three periods according to grade level. The first recess period consisted of second and fourth graders, the second consisted of first and third graders, and the third consisted of fifth and sixth graders. Kindergarten recess overlapped between first and second recess periods; therefore, behavior counts for kindergarten students could potentially appear in the first and second recess periods. Each recess period was approximately 15 to 20 minutes in length. Pairs of staff, one a certified teacher and the other a paraprofessional, provided supervision during each recess period. At times across the study, an additional paraprofessional would assist with supervision. The inclusion of the additional supervisor did not follow a predictable pattern.

Procedure and Design

The target school was involved in an ongoing process of developing a schoolwide system of positive behavior support prior to and during the study (Lewis & Sugai, 1999). A school team was formed to (a) assess the current school environment, specifically the schoolwide and non-classroom systems of support, (b) develop instructional interventions targeting identified areas of concern, (c) develop reinforcement procedures to promote student success, and (d) develop staff procedures to ensure integrity of implementation. As a result of a school system assessment (Lewis & Sugai, 1999), the school developed a common set of schoolwide rules (be kind, be safe, be cooperative, be respectful, be peaceful, be responsible) and established and implemented a reinforcement system to acknowledge student mastery. Although this system was successful in improving general school behavior, as noted by decreases in office referrals, students' playground behavior remained an area of concern.

Following development of the schoolwide system, the team applied the same assessment and problem-solving process to the playground. Planning activities included (a) assessing the current and needed setting routines, (b) assessing the physical environment, (c) identifying desired behavior, and (d) developing instructional strategies and needed support structures (Garrison-Harrell & Lewis, 1999). Based on assessment information, the team with the authors' assistance developed the intervention described in detail below.

A multiple baseline across setting design was used (Tawney & Gast, 1984). Following three baseline sessions, intervention began during recess one. Intervention consisted of social skill instruction occurring in the classroom and on the playground and a group contingency. Following completion of 10 days of social skill instruction during recess period one, intervention began with the second cohort of grades that made up recess two. Likewise, intervention began in recess three following the completion of instruction for grades that attended recess two.

Intervention

The intervention consisted of two components: (a) teaching rules, routines, and desired behavior, and (b) a group contingency.

Teaching rules, routines, and desired behavior.   Members of the school team, with the assistance of the authors, developed social skill lessons that used the existing set of schoolwide expectations. For each school rule, specific behaviors appropriate for the playground were identified. In addition, common problem behaviors were used in the lesson as "nonexamples" of school expectations. Lessons were designed to (a) define the rule, (b) provide examples of the rule, (c) model the expected behavior, (d) have students practice expected behavior, and (e) review and test (Sugai & Lewis, 1996). Nine lessons—six addressing rules and routines for specific activities and games (tether ball, basketball, four square, kickball, soccer, and activity center) and three for desired social skills (how to join a game or activity, how to win and lose a game, and how to line up when the bell rings)—were developed.

Following lesson development, the school team taught their colleagues to use the social skill lessons by modeling sample lessons and reviewing the written lesson plans. All classroom teachers then taught the nine lessons over a 2-week period in their classrooms. In addition, all classroom teachers reviewed and practiced the skills at least twice on the playground during nonrecess periods.

Group contingency.   The second component consisted of implementing a token group contingency system within each of the recess periods. The purpose of the playground reinforcement system was twofold; first, to encourage the staff to acknowledge students at high rates for displaying appropriate behavior; and second, to increase student use of appropriate and decrease use of inappropriate social skills. Playground monitors carried elastic loops and gave them to students who were complying with targeted social skills. Students could place the loops on their wrists to avoid losing them. Upon returning to the classroom from the playground, students placed their loops in a can on the teacher's desk. While placing the loops in the can, teachers were instructed to ask the students why they earned the loops. Once the can was full, each classroom voted on a group contingency. Examples of group contingencies classes elected included earning extra recess, using the loops themselves to make things, and receiving candy. Several classes were able to earn multiple contingencies during the course of the study.

Targeted Behaviors

Frequency counts of problem behavior were collected during a 10-minute period within each recess session. Six problem behaviors were identified and defined by the school team. Behaviors and their operational definitions are presented in Table 1.

Data Collection

Daily probe session data were collected using a frequency count paper and pencil format. Data were collected during random days across school weeks from March through May. At least two data points were collected per school week and data were distributed across the school week such that each day was represented and had an equal opportunity of being randomly selected. A probe versus continuous schedule was selected due to the applied nature of the study. School personnel, who were not available on a consistent daily basis, collected all data. Two data collectors were present during all recess periods collecting data for the 10-minute period. Data collection started once the majority of children were on the playground. One data collector focused on "structured" recess activities while the second focused on "unstructured" recess activities (Lewis et al., 2000). Structured recess activities were defined as those that had clear rules (e.g., basketball, tetherball). Unstructured recess activities were defined as those that had no clear rules (e.g., playing on the jungle gym). Analysis of the raw data indicated no discernable patterns across struc-

Table 1
Target behavior and operational definitions

Behavior	Definition and Example of Behavior
Hands on Others/Pushing	Putting hands on others in an aggressive manner, including pushing, shoving, bumping, hitting, kicking, pulling, and wrestling. Examples: Pushing way into line, swinging coats and hitting each other. Exclusion: Socially appropriate touch such as walking arm and arm, holding hands with friends, incidental contact that is part of a game such as two players colliding in soccer when passing the ball.
Misuse of Equipment	Any use of equipment in a manner other than what it was designed for or rules for intended use. Examples: Standing on or climbing up slide, stopping on slide, going wrong way on rings, running under rings when students are using rings, twisting swings, lying on swings, kicking basketball, tying people up with jumprope, swinging jumprope at people, jumping out of swings, and hanging on tetherball.
Language/Name Calling	Use of profanity, name calling, insults, put downs, slurs, teasing, and inappropriate gestures.
Interfering With Activity	Interrupting activity already in progress. Examples: grabbing the basketball during a game, grabbing and holding swing while someone is swinging, holding ball/equipment to stop the game or activity, and walking or running through activity.
Arguing More Than 10 Seconds	Continuing with an argument for longer than 10 seconds. Examples: Arguing with official's call, arguing over whose turn it is.
Playing With Rocks	Playing in rocks including digging, throwing, or kicking rocks. Exclusion: Walking on rocks

tured and unstructured observations, and the data were therefore collapsed into a single data point per recess.

Prior to starting data collection, data collectors observed during nontargeted recess to (a) build reliability, (b) refine behavior definitions, (c) develop observation routines, and (d) desensitize the students to their presence. Training continued until observers reached at least 80% interobserver agreement.

Informal observations were also made on implementation integrity of the procedures on the playground. Feedback was given to the behavior support team to refine implementation. A lead teacher from the team assisted the playground monitors by directly teaching and modeling procedures. Overall, reports indicate that playground monitors were prompting and reinforcing students at an appropriate level.

Interobserver Agreement

A third observer conducted interobserver agreement checks throughout the study. Interobserver agreement checks occurred across 38% of the data collection sessions. Percent agreement was calculated by dividing the two frequency totals and multiplying by 100. Interobserver agreement averaged 93% (range, 86–100%).

RESULTS

Daily counts of problem behavior were aggregated for each recess session into a single data point, plotted, and visually analyzed for within- and between-phase differences (see Fig. 1). A

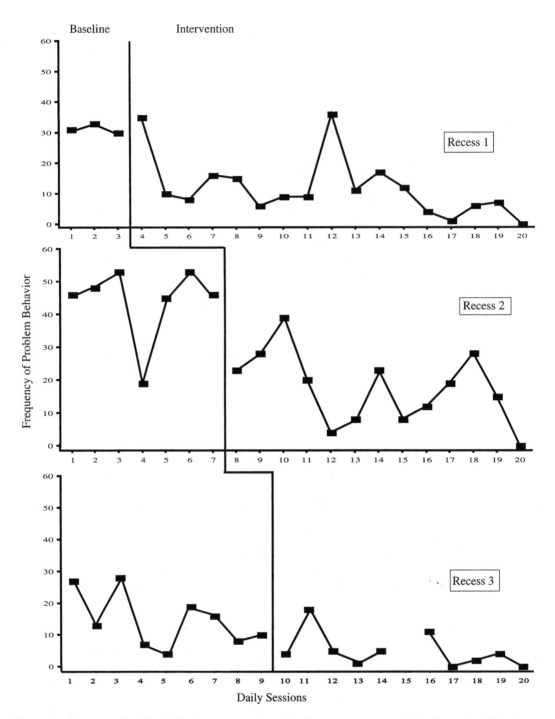

FIGURE 1.   Frequency of problem behavior across recess periods. Recess one was comprised of second- and fourth-grade students, recess two was comprised of first- and third-grade students, and recess three was comprised of fifth- and sixth-grade students. Kindergarten students were on the playground across recess periods one and two.

"split-middle" procedure was used to determine trend lines (White & Haring, 1980) stability was determined if 80% or more of the data points fell within a range of 15% of mean level (Tawney & Gast, 1984), and across-phase level changes were determined by visual inspection (Tawney & Gast, 1984).

Baseline data indicate a level trend during recess one (mean 31.3, range 30–33), a slightly decreasing trend but overall high frequency during recess two (mean 44.3, range 19–53), and a decreasing trend with overall low frequency during recess three (mean 13.6, range 4–28). During intervention, data indicate level changes for recess one (mean 11.8, range 0–36) and two (mean 17.5, range 0–39) with decreasing trends. Recess three (mean 5.1, range 0–18) shows a slight level change with a flat trend line. Overall results suggest that the intervention did impact the frequency of problem behavior observed on the playground, especially during recesses one and two. For recess three, the initial low frequency and decreasing trend limit our ability to make firm statements regarding the functional relationship between the intervention and the outcome. Long-term outcome data were not collected due to the fact the study ended with the school year.

DISCUSSION

The purpose of this study was to evaluate the effectiveness of an applied intervention consisting of social skill instruction and group contingencies on the frequency of problem behavior displayed by elementary students on the playground. The results indicate that the teachers and support staff were successful in reducing frequency of problem behavior. In addition to the applied outcome of the study, the results make several contributions to the emerging knowledge base on the effectiveness of schoolwide systems of PBS.

Implications for Practice

The present study adds to the growing base of empirical evidence supporting the use of universal PBS strategies to reduce problem behaviors (Colvin et al., 1997; Lewis et al., 1998; Scott, 2001; Taylor-Green & Kartub, 2000; Taylor-Greene et al., 1997). The present study adds to this growing base in several important ways. First, the present study was conducted within a school that is typically considered challenging or "at risk" due to several factors such as large numbers of children coming from poverty and large numbers of minority students. Second, the large number of students who leave and enter throughout the school year also creates behavior concerns. While the overall number of students within the target school remains fairly constant, by mid school year, approximately 50% of the students enrolled did not start the school year in this school. While the study was running, several children left and several enrolled. The consistent, positive instruction-based focus of universal PBS strategies used in this study clearly provided a context in which new students could reach fluency with the behavior expectations even though they were not part of the traditional review of expectations at the start of the school year. Third, all of the intervention procedures described in this study were developed and implemented by school personnel. The only external support came from district behavior consultants. The behavior consultants assisted with lesson development and were responsible for data collection.

One of the larger purposes of this study was to extend the target school's system of PBS across nonclassroom settings. Through a relatively simple, non-intrusive instructional-based intervention, educators were able to reduce problem behaviors on the playground. However, results presented in this study cannot be viewed in isolation; rather, they should be viewed within the larger schoolwide efforts. This is especially salient as schools attempt to replicate the present study in an effort to address their behavior challenges. Several components must be considered as possible influencing factors with respect to the present studies' findings. First, prior to addressing the problems observed during recess, the school had implemented a schoolwide set of expectations for several months. The frequent use of a common set of school expectations and a larger schoolwide reinforcement system may have "primed" the students to be more receptive to the playground intervention. Second, the school had also developed and implemented a similar PBS strategy to address problem behavior in the cafeteria. The success in the cafeteria may also have influenced both student and adult behavior, leading to the present outcomes. Finally, while the school set the agenda to implement the present study, technical assistance was available to assist in the process through behavior consultants. In addition to expertise in behavior and instructional management, the consultants also had expertise and experience in developing schoolwide systems of PBS. Each of these factors have implications for practice and future research in that each are identified as essential features in current recommendations (Sugai et al., 2000).

Implications for Research

The present study provides further support for the effectiveness of social skills programs paired with generalization strategies. Recently, the efficacy of social skills instruction as a strategy to reduce problem behavior has been questioned (e.g., Mathur, Kavale, Quinn, Forness, & Rutherford, 1998). The efficacy debate has largely been due to the outcomes of recent statistical meta-analyses of a database that is primarily comprised of single-subject studies (Gresham, 1998). As pointed out by Gresham, Sugai, and Horner (2001), the debate would serve the field better by examining the context in which social skill training occurs and what variables are functionally related to successful outcomes. The present study provides at least a modest level of support for the use of social skill training across students with and without disabilities. More importantly, the results of this study have demonstrated positive effects across 450 students when instruction occurred within the context of a larger school system in which all students and staff were fluent with common school expectations and related social skills. The results of social skill instruction alone cannot be determined since the intervention paired training with a group contingency. However, the applied pairing of the two further speaks to the importance of contextualizing social skill instruction and building in generalization strategies, such as group contingencies, from the start (Gresham et al., 2001).

A second important outcome of this study is the collection of further data to support the need for a complete continuum of PBS (Sugai et al., 2000). While the data show reductions across each recess period, the frequency of problem behavior does not drop to zero. An anecdotal review of the raw data, with input from the playground supervisors, once again confirms the fact that while universal strategies met the needs of the majority of students, they were not sufficient to support students who display chronic patterns of problem behavior (Sugai & Horner, 1994). However, by building in universal strategies, this school and others are better able to implement small group and individual student interventions within existing time and resource constraints. For example, the present study showed a reduction of a mean level of 30 problem behaviors during baseline to a mean level of 12 during intervention across all three recess periods. Reducing the overall number of problem behaviors school personnel must address allows them more time to reinforce students who are engaging in appropriate behavior and focus on specific students and problem areas. Similar outcomes have been observed in other research. For example, Scott (2001), using universal PBS strategies, demonstrated that by reducing the amount of time students spent in detention, the school gained an additional 761 hours of in-class instruction time. Viewed another way, the school is not using a staff member's time to supervise 761 hours of in-school detention. By reducing supervision of detention, a resource can now be used more proactively such as working with small groups and individual students.

Limitations

Given the applied nature of the present study, a number of limitations have been identified. First, the specific factor that impacted student behavior cannot be determined as both social skill instruction and group contingencies were implemented simultaneously. Second, while informal checks were made to insure that classroom teachers and playground supervisors were implementing the intervention as designed, such as making sure all teachers were teaching the requisite days, all taught at least two lessons on the playground, and playground supervisors were distributing the "loops," no formal integrity checks occurred. Future research including (a) implementation checks such as insuring all lesson components were covered daily, (b) student acquisition checks, and (c) rate of contingency delivery would provide more insight with respect to assessing efficacy. A final limitation is the overall weak effect observed in recess three. Due to a very low baseline level observed, intervention effects were minimal. However, intervention data did show a decreasing trend. This overall low level in recess three may have been due to several factors such as the age of the students (i.e., the oldest group) or the fact that they were more fluent with expectations due to longer learning histories with the schoolwide system. Future research is needed to examine the specific factors related to the observed outcome and if they are typical of other elementary school playgrounds.

CONCLUSION

Through the use of simple instructional and reinforcement strategies, this study has demonstrated that schools can impact problem behavior. This is especially encouraging given the demographic makeup (i.e., large numbers of students from impoverished backgrounds) and the transient nature of a large percentage of the school population, two factors that place any school "at risk" for significant problem behavior. By creating contexts in which problem behavior is reduced through positive strategies as opposed to punishment, corollary outcomes such as improvements in school climate, teacher confidence to address problem behavior, and a reallocation of resources were observed. Clearly, future research and additional applied evaluations are warranted to continue to add and expand the current knowledge base to support the use of a continuum of PBS in school settings. Specifically, more detailed and controlled studies are needed to isolate essential features that lead to positive outcomes. In addition, more replications are needed across diverse school populations.

REFERENCES

Colvin, G., & Lowe, R. (1986). Getting good recess supervision isn't child's play. Executive Educator, 8, 20–21.

Colvin, G., Sugai, G., Good, R.H. III, & Lee, Y. (1997). Using active supervision and precorrection to improve transition behaviors in an elementary school. School Psychology Quarterly, 12, 344–363.

Dwyer, K., & Osher, D. (2000). Safeguarding our children: An action guide. Washington, DC: U.S. Departments of Education and Justice, American Institutes for Research.

Dwyer, K., Osher, D., & Warger, C. (1998). Early warning, timely response: A guide to safe schools. Washington, DC: U.S. Department of Education.

Garrison-Harrell, L., & Lewis, T.J. (1999). Extending school-wide systems of support to nonclassroom settings. In T.J. Lewis & G. Sugai (Eds.), Safe schools: School-wide discipline practices (pp. 13–18). Reston, VA: Council for Exceptional Children.

Gresham, F.M. (1998). Social skills training: Should we raze, remodel, or rebuild? Behavioral Disorders, 24, 19–25.

Gresham, F.M., Sugai, G., & Horner, R.H. (2001). Interpreting outcomes of social skill training for students with high-incidence disabilities. Exceptional Children, 67, 331–344.

Hendricks, C.M. (1993). Safer playgrounds for young children. Washington, DC: ERIC Clearing House on Teacher Education.

Kartub, D.T., Taylor-Greene, S., March, R.E., & Horner, R.H. (2000). Reducing hallway noise: A systems approach. Journal of Positive Behavior Interventions, 2, 179–182.

Lewis, T.J., Colvin, G., & Sugai, G. (2000). The effects of precorrection and active supervision on the recess behavior of elementary school students. Education and Treatment of Children, 23, 109–121.

Lewis, T.J., & Sugai, G. (1999). Effective behavior support: A systems approach to proactive school-wide management. Focus on Exceptional Children, 31, 1–24.

Lewis, T.J., Sugai, G., & Colvin, G. (1998). Reducing problem behavior through a school-side system of effective behavioral support: Investigation of a school-wide social skills training program and contextual interventions. School Psychology Review, 27, 446–459.

Mathur, S., Kavale, K., Quinn, M., Forness, S., & Rutherford, R. (1998). Social skills intervention with students with emotional and behavioral problems: A quantitative synthesis of single subject research. Behavioral Disorders, 23, 193–201.

Nakasato, J. (2000). Data-based decision making in Hawaii's behavior support effort. Journal of Positive Behavioral Interventions, 2, 247–251.

Scott, T.M. (2001). A school-wide example of positive behavioral support. Journal of Positive Behavioral Interventions, 3, 88–94.

Sugai, G., & Horner, R. (1994). Including students with severe behavior problems in general education settings: Assumptions, challenges, and solutions. In J. Marr, G. Sugai, & G. Tindal (Eds.). The Oregon conference monograph (Vol. 6) (pp. 102–120). Eugene, OR: University of Oregon.

Sugai, G., Horner, R.H., Dunlap, G., Hieneman, M., Lewis, T.J., Nelson, C.M., Scott, T., Liaupsin, C., Sailor, W., Turnbull, A., Turnbull, H.R., Wickham, D., Wicox, B., & Ruef, M. (2000). Applying positive behavior support and functional behavioral assessment in schools. Journal of Positive Behavior Interventions, 2, 131–143.

Sugai, G., & Lewis, T. (1996). Preferred and promising practices for social skill instruction. Focus on Exceptional Children, 29, 1–16.

Tawney, J.W., & Gast, D.L. (1984). Single subject research in special education. Columbus, OH: Merrill.

Taylor-Green, S., Brown, D., Nelson, L., Longton, J., Gassman, T., Cohen, J., Swartz, J., Horner, R.H., Sugai, G., & Hall, S. (1997). School-wide behavioral support: Starting the year off right. Journal of Behavioral Education, 7, 99–112.

Taylor-Greene, S.J., & Kartub, D.T. (2000). Durable implementation of school-wide behavior support: The high five program. Journal of Positive Behavioral Interventions, 2, 233–235.

Thompson, T. (1991). People make a difference in school playground safety. Executive Educator, 13, 28–29.

U.S. Department of Education (1998). Violence and discipline problems in U.S. public schools: 1996–97. Washington, DC: U.S. Department of Education, National Center for Educational Statistics.

U.S. Department of Education (2000). Prevention research and the IDEA discipline provisions: A guide for school administrators. Washington, DC: Author.

U.S. Public Health Service (2000). Report of the surgeon general's conference on children's mental health: A national action agenda. Washington, DC: Author.

White, O.R., & Haring, N.G. (1980). Exceptional teaching (2nd ed.). Columbus, OH: Merrill.

Psychology in the Schools, Vol. 39(2), 2002
© 2002 Wiley Periodicals, Inc.

DOI: 10.1002/pits.10030

ALTERING EDUCATIONAL ENVIRONMENTS THROUGH POSITIVE PEER REPORTING: PREVENTION AND REMEDIATION OF SOCIAL PROBLEMS ASSOCIATED WITH BEHAVIOR DISORDERS

CHRISTOPHER H. SKINNER AND CHRISTINE E. NEDDENRIEP

University of Tennessee

SHERI L. ROBINSON

University of Texas–Austin

RUTH ERVIN

Western Michigan University

KEVIN JONES

University of Cincinnati

Typical classroom management procedures designed to reduce instances of inappropriate social behavior (i.e., tattling and punishment systems) may adversely impact the social development and social relations of students with behavior and/or social emotional disorders. Two alternative procedures where students are encouraged to monitor and report incidental prosocial behaviors are described and research supporting their effectiveness in remedying and preventing social interaction problems within classroom environments are reviewed. Recommendations for future research on altering classroom environments so that peers encourage and support classmates' incidental prosocial behavior are provided. © 2002 Wiley Periodicals, Inc.

Within educational environments, punitive systems have been designed to prevent students from engaging in incidental antisocial behaviors. These systems often take the form of rules that identify unacceptable behaviors and specify consequences and processes for delivering those consequences contingent upon those behaviors (Skinner, Cashwell, & Skinner, 2000). Typically, these systems are independent group contingencies. The group aspect of the contingency indicates that each individual receives the same consequence (i.e., punishment) contingent upon the same antisocial behavior (Hayes, 1976; Litow & Pumroy, 1975). The independent aspect signifies that students are punished for their own behavior, rather than their peers' behavior. These characteristics of rules address concerns about fairness and equal protection, and make students responsible for their own behavior (Skinner, Skinner, Skinner, & Cashwell, 1999).

In many instances, these punitive systems may be effective in preventing students from engaging in incidental inappropriate behaviors. However, as with any contingency, these independent group punishment procedures are not equally effective across all children (Iwata, Dorsey, Slifer, Bauman, & Richman, 1994). When specific children persist in engaging in incidental antisocial behaviors, despite these punitive systems, they may be referred for psycho-educational assessment and diagnosed as having behavior or social-emotional disorders. Thus, in some cases, children with behavior or social-emotional disorders are children who engage in high rates of incidental antisocial behavior under environmental conditions designed to punish those behaviors.

In this article, punitive systems designed to prevent antisocial behavior are described and analyzed. After discussing possible negative side effects associated with using peers to monitor and report incidental antisocial behavior of their classmates with behavior disorders, the focus shifts to procedures designed to encourage incidental prosocial behavior. Methods, theory, and research related to two procedures that encourage peers to monitor and report classmates' appro-

Correspondence to: Christopher H. Skinner, University of Tennessee, College of Education, 438 Claxton Addition, Knoxville, TN 37996-3400. E-mail: cskinne1@utk.edu

priate prosocial behaviors are reviewed and analyzed. Finally, directions for future applied and theoretical research are provided.

Peer Participation With Independent Group Punishment: Tattling

One problem associated with punishing antisocial behavior is that educators often have difficulty monitoring antisocial behavior. Because incidental antisocial behaviors are often punished, one way to avoid punishment is to avoid detection. Hence, students may still engage in these antisocial behaviors, but learn to avoid being caught. In this manner, merely punishing antisocial behaviors can teach children to avoid detection and be sneaky, rather than to behave prosocially (LaVigna & Donnellan, 1986).

Because it is not possible for teachers to monitor each student's behavior, students help with this task by observing and monitoring their peers' behavior and reporting inappropriate behaviors to authority figures, (i.e., tattling). This entire system, based on peer monitoring and reporting of classmates' incidental inappropriate behaviors (i.e., tattling), seems to have evolved in a similar manner in diverse education environments (Henington & Skinner, 1998).

Social Side Effects of Punishment and Tattling on Students With Behavior Disorders

Research suggests that teachers spend more time focused on and responding to inappropriate as opposed to appropriate behaviors (Thomas, Presland, Grant, & Glynn, 1978; White, 1975). By encouraging students to monitor and report peers' incidental antisocial behavior, tattling and punishment procedures may have a similar effect on students. This may cause social problems for students with behavior or social-emotional disorders who may engage in higher rates of these incidental antisocial behaviors than their peers. Specifically, encouraging peers to monitor and report *only* incidental antisocial behaviors may inadvertently cause classmates to ignore prosocial behaviors of students with behavior or emotional disorders. Consequently, peers' perceptions of classmates with social-emotional or behavior disorders may be inaccurate, unbalanced, and harsh because they are based primarily on inappropriate behaviors (Henington & Skinner, 1998). In this manner, tattling and punishment systems may encourage students to socially reject or neglect peers with behavior disorders.

Research examining peer rejection has typically utilized classroom sociometric measures, asking children to nominate peers whom they like the most and peers whom they like the least (Asher & Dodge, 1986; Terry & Coie, 1991). Children receiving a high number of liked-least nominations and a low number of liked-most nominations are considered rejected. Students who receive few nominations (either liked-least or liked-most) are considered neglected. Those students who demonstrate aggressive, withdrawn, or inattentive-hyperactive behaviors are more likely to be rejected (Dodge, Coie, Petit, & Price, 1990; Newcomb, Bukowski, & Pattee, 1993). Also, those students who are socially rejected and/or neglected by peers are more likely to experience other school-related problems, engage in delinquent behavior, and experience mental health problems (Coie, Dodge, & Kupersmidt, 1990; Parker & Asher, 1987). Furthermore, the additive effect of both aggression and peer rejection in boys has been shown to produce the poorest outcome in adolescence (Bierman & Wargo, 1995; Coie, Lochman, Terry, & Hyman, 1992; Coie, Terry, Lenox, Lochman, & Hyman, 1995).

Many students who are rejected or neglected by peers may repeatedly experience their peers' rejection over time, despite changes in peer groups (Bukowski & Newcomb, 1984; Coie & Dodge, 1983). Coie and Dodge (1983) found that almost half the children rejected in fifth grade continued to be rejected over a 5-year period. Thus, peer rejection may be persistent and children may continue to reject some children despite changes in the student's behavior over time (Coie &

Cillessen, 1993). In addition, the emotional impact of peer rejection detrimentally increases as the peers' rejection is persistently experienced over time (DeRosier, Kupersmidt, & Patterson, 1994).

SOCIAL SKILLS MASTERY

School psychologists, educators, teachers, and counselors have tried different strategies and procedures to enhance the social interactions of students with behavior disorders. Perhaps the most common procedure is to teach students appropriate prosocial behaviors. Researchers have developed social skills curricula that are designed to teach appropriate social behaviors (see Stumbo, 1995). Additionally, some teachers develop and plan their own lessons designed to teach prosocial behaviors such as sharing, waiting their turn, and asking for and/or giving help.

Researchers who reviewed studies on social skills training have found that such procedures are effective for teaching students appropriate social behaviors; however, few have shown that such procedures alter students' incidental social behaviors within their natural environment (DuPaul & Ekert, 1994; Forness & Kavale, 1996; Ogilvy, 1994). There are several reasons why social skills training programs may not result in improved social behavior within natural environments. One limitation of most social skills training programs is that they focus primarily on skill acquisition. In many cases, children with behavior disorders may have already acquired social skills. Thus programs that are designed to teach skills may be addressing the wrong problem (Gresham, 1995). Acquisition is merely the first stage of skill learning. If skills are to be functional, students must maintain those skills, become fluent with those skills, be able to generalize those skills to appropriate natural environments, and adapt those skills as environmental contingencies change (Haring & Eaton, 1978).

Opportunities to practice acquired skills have been shown to be effective and may be necessary to enhance skill fluency and maintenance (Binder, 1996; Skinner, 1998). When these opportunities to practice acquired skills occur in natural environments, then generalization and adaptation may be enhanced. This is particularly important with respect to social skills mastery. Because social environments are fluid and cues are subtle it is difficult to identify behaviors that will consistently be reinforced, punished, or ignored across social settings and over time. For example, interrupting a speaker with a funny remark may yield social reinforcement (e.g., laughter) in some situations, while in other subtly different situations such behavior may be socially punished. Thus, successful use of social skills requires students to constantly alter their behavior based on subtle and perhaps difficult to discriminate differences across social situations.

Because it is difficult to identify and teach behaviors that are appropriate across complex, fluid, and subtly different social situations, many social skills are mastered through day-to-day social interactions where peers and others shape social behaviors. In this incidental manner, students may develop and master social skills. However, in order to do this, children need opportunities to engage in social behaviors within their natural social environments, and they must choose to engage in these social interactions. Further, in order for these behaviors to be maintained, they must be supported/reinforced in the natural settings in which they occur.

Unfortunately, research suggests that students who are rejected or neglected (e.g., students who are aggressive, withdrawn, or hyperactive) may receive fewer opportunities to develop their social skills within natural incidental social situations. For example Ladd, Price, and Hart (1990) showed that negative peer nominations at the beginning of the school year predicted less peer contacts at midyear. Similarly, negative nominations at midyear predicted fewer peer contacts at the year's end. Thus, these students who need more exposure to natural social learning situations in order to develop and master social skills may actually receive fewer opportunities to have their social skills shaped through incidental learning. This lack of social interaction can adversely impact on the development and mastery of social skills, thereby hindering the students' ability to establish subsequent social relationships (Stormshak et al., 1999).

There are several reasons why students with behavior disorders may have few incidental social interactions with peers. First, classmates may find that social interactions with students who are withdrawn, hyperactive, aggressive, or inattentive are aversive or less rewarding than interactions with other peers (Stormshak et al., 1999). Thus, peers may avoid social interactions with students who have behavior or emotional disorders (McDowell, 1988; Myerson & Hale, 1984). Additionally, students with behavior or emotional disorders may avoid interactions with peers. Students who are rejected or neglected are likely to have a history of their social behaviors being punished (e.g., rejected students) or extinguished (e.g., neglected children). In some instances, these naturally occurring aversive consequences for antisocial behaviors may be useful in that they reduce the probability of students engaging in further antisocial behaviors. However, in other instances, students may avoid these aversive social consequences by failing to initiate social interactions and withdrawing from or avoiding social situations. When neglected or rejected students avoid social situations, they lose opportunities to develop and master complex social skills (e.g., discriminating when a sarcastic remark is funny versus when such behavior is likely to be ignored or punished).

Segregating students with behavior or social emotional disorders may make matters worse because peers may encourage or shape atypical social behavior. For example, in a self-contained classroom serving students with behavior disorders, aggressive behavior may be reinforced by peers (Boivin, Dodge, & Coie, 1995; Wright, Giammarino, & Parad, 1986). However, peers may ignore or socially punish these same behaviors within general education environments.

Encouraging Incidental Prosocial Behaviors

While preventing and decreasing inappropriate behaviors is an important goal in any school system, schools are not meeting their educational goals if inappropriate behaviors are not replaced with appropriate behaviors (Winette & Winkler, 1972). Merely helping students acquire appropriate social behaviors is unlikely to be sufficient to prevent or alleviate social problems, unless those behaviors are supported in their natural environments (Gresham, 1995).

Incidental Learning: Taking Advantage of the Situation

Incidental opportunities for teaching and shaping appropriate prosocial behaviors often occur in educational environments (Cashwell, Skinner, & Smith, in press). For example, a student may notice that a peer's pen has run out of ink. Without prompting, the student quietly offers the classmate one of her/his extra pens. An unplanned, incidental prosocial behavior has just occurred. Although the teacher could have used this incidental event as a learning experience for the students involved and their peers, there are several reasons why this opportunity to praise, reinforce, encourage, and/or teach these appropriate prosocial behaviors is often lost.

The most basic reason why the previously mentioned prosocial behavior (i.e., offer a peer a pen) could not be used as an incidental learning experience is because the teacher did not directly observe the prosocial behavior. In many instances, teachers may not directly observe prosocial student-helping-student behaviors. Even when teachers directly observe prosocial behaviors, they may not be aware or cognizant of these behaviors. Teachers often spend so much time and cognitive energy monitoring students' inappropriate behaviors that they may not be aware of all the incidental prosocial behaviors that occur during daily classroom activities. (Algozzine, 1980; Reisberg, Fudell, & Hudson, 1982; Thomas et al., 1978; White, 1975).

In some instances, educators who observe and are cognizant of incidental instances of non-dramatic prosocial behaviors intentionally ignore the behaviors. In many cases these adults feel that students are supposed to behave in an altruistic manner and should not be reinforced for doing what is expected, or for "doing what they are supposed to be doing" (Hall, 1991; O'Leary, Poulos, & Devine, 1972; Pumroy & McIntire, 1991). This is unfortunate, as a large and convincing body of research suggests that reinforcing behaviors within natural environments is an effective and often necessary procedure to promote and maintain social behaviors (see Kazdin, 2001 or Wielkiewicz, 1995).

A final problem with the previously described scenario is that, even if the teacher did observe the appropriate behavior and reinforce the student for helping her/his classmate, other students may not learn from this event. Punishing students who misbehave may suppress misbehavior rates in other students (Bandura, 1977). In a similar vein, reinforcing students for behaving prosocially may increase prosocial behaviors in other students (Cashwell et al., 2001). However, this learning is unlikely to occur if other students are not informed of, or do not directly observe, their peers' appropriate behaviors and the related reinforcing event.

Positive Peer Reporting and Tootling

Beginning in their early school years, without formal instruction, students learn to monitor and report incidental instances of peers' inappropriate behaviors (i.e., tattle). If students can learn at an early age to monitor and report peers' inappropriate behaviors, then they could learn to monitor and report appropriate prosocial behaviors.

Grieger, Kaufman, and Grieger (1976) published the first study in a line of research documenting the benefits of having peers report prosocial behaviors of other peers. In this first study, kindergarten teachers told their students (90 participants) that they would be given an opportunity to name one student who had done something nice for them during play period. Students who were named were then allowed to select a happy face. Providing opportunities for peers to report prosocial behaviors resulted in increased cooperative play and decreased aggression.

Next, two promising peer-reporting procedures will be described that may encourage students to focus on and report their peers incidental prosocial behaviors. The first procedure, positive peer reporting (PPR), has been shown to be effective in altering the social status of students with behavior disorders and enhancing the quality and quantity of social interactions in these students.

The second procedure, tootling, is designed for classwide implementation. The tootling and PPR programs described are based on similar assumptions. PPR is based on the assumption that some students with social interaction problems may have acquired appropriate social skills (e.g., they engage in appropriate social behaviors), but may be ostracized by their peers because they engage in these behaviors less frequently than their peers. Thus, the goal of the program was to enhance reinforcement for prosocial behaviors by having peers publicly acknowledge those appropriate behaviors that were already occurring in the students' natural environments. Furthermore, it was hoped that public acknowledgement would alter peers' perceptions of targeted students.

The tootling program is based on the assumption that peers spend so much time monitoring classmates' socially inappropriate behavior that they may not be aware of, respond to (e.g., socially reinforce), or value incidental prosocial behavior. Thus, this program is designed to enhance classroom environments by increasing the probability that peers will engage in incidental student-helping-student behaviors and also increase their awareness of and appreciation for these behaviors.

Positive peer reporting (PPR). PPR is a relatively simple procedure that has been used in residential and educational settings to enhance peer interactions and peers' perceptions of students who are socially rejected or neglected (Bowers, McGinnis, Ervin, & Friman, 1999; Bowers, Woods, Carlyon, & Friman, 2000; Ervin, Johnston, & Friman, 1998; Ervin, Miller, & Friman, 1996; Jones,

Young, & Friman, 2000; Robinson, 1998). Table 1 provides a basic outline of the procedure. Instead of reporting inappropriate instances of behavior, children are told they will have the opportunity to earn reinforcement (e.g., tokens) for noticing and reporting a peer's positive behavior. The procedures are then explained to the students. First, a target student is randomly selected as the "Star of the Week." During a specified time of day (e.g., last 10 minutes of homeroom), a group session is held where peers are given the opportunity to report aloud any positive behaviors they observed from this student that day. Students typically require training with practice and feedback in order to learn to identify examples of positive behaviors (e.g., Billy shared his soccer ball at recess). The behaviors reported must be deemed by the teacher as specific and genuine in order for the child reporting the behavior to receive reinforcement.

Ervin et al. (1996) used PPR to improve the social interactions and acceptance of a 13-year-old socially rejected girl in a residential treatment setting. The procedure consisted of classmates reporting positive behaviors of the target child to the teacher (but with the target child present) during the last 5 minutes of math class. Peers' positive comments were awarded points that could be exchanged later for tangible or activity reinforcement. Efficacy of the procedure was evaluated using an ABAB design where positive and negative peer interactions within the residential setting served as the primary dependent measures. Additionally, peer ratings were collected as a measure of sociometric status. Results showed that PPR decreased negative and increased positive social interactions with peers. Additionally, peers rated this student more favorably following the intervention.

Table 1
Step-by-Step Procedure for Positive Peer Reporting

1. Introduce and define positive peer reporting (PPR).
   PPR is the opposite of tattling.
   Students will be given the chance to earn reinforcement (e.g., points, activities) for reporting positive behaviors of peers.

2. Explain the procedure.
   A drawing will be conducted and a child's name will be selected as the first target child (e.g., "Star of the Week").
   Peers will be instructed to pay special attention to the target child's positive behaviors during the course of the day and to report the observed incidences of positive behaviors during the specified time of day.
   Positive comments include behaviors like sharing, helping a friend, volunteering, showing good anger control, honesty, trying hard in school, giving others praise, encouragement or compliments, or any behavior that is specific target area for the target child (e.g., asking for help instead of giving up).
   The teacher determines that the report of positive behavior is specific and genuine, and the child reporting the behavior receives the identified reinforcement.
   A child will be the target child for 1 week and then there will be a new drawing for the next "Star of the Week."

3. Determine the type and amount of reinforcement that will be given for reports of positive behavior (e.g., special activity, points, tokens for previously established token economy system).

4. Determine the time of day and amount of time allotted for the procedure (e.g., during the last 10 minutes of homeroom peers will be given the opportunity to report any instances of positive behaviors they witnessed the target child exhibit that day).

5. Monitor the effects of the intervention on the quality of peer interactions by coding interactions (e.g., positive, negative or neutral). Monitor the effects of the intervention on social status using peer ratings and nominations.

Subsequent studies conducted at Boys Town investigated the effects of similar interventions (Bowers et al., 1999; Bowers et al., 2000; Robinson, 1998). Across these three investigations, there were nine target students. Data suggest that the PPR procedure or a modified version of this procedure increased the percentage of positive interactions with peers for all nine target students and enhanced peers' perceptions of target students for eight of the nine target students. Additionally, Bowers et al. (1999) found that a modified PPR procedure decreased negative peer interaction rates.

Researchers also investigated the effects of PPR on social initiation and cooperative statements. Robinson (1998) found that PPR increased target students' rates of initiating social interactions with peers. However, the peers who provided the positive reports did not increase their social initiations with target students. Jones et al. (2000) evaluated the effects of PPR on students' cooperative statements. Target students were three children from the middle school who were identified by their mathematics teacher as rejected. Three times per week, cooperative learning groups of three were formed to complete math assignments. Following cooperative learning activities, 5-minute sessions were held where peers provided the target child with positive comments about behaviors and the target child was encouraged to provide three reciprocal comments to peers. During cooperative mathematics activities, all three participants' mean percentage of cooperative statements increased during intervention phases, with median peer acceptance ratings also increasing from preintervention to postintervention.

Another study was conducted in a general education elementary school classroom to evaluate the effectiveness of PPR on the social interactions of a socially rejected 6-year-old girl (Ervin et al., 1998). In order to accommodate the age of the participants, the classroom teacher altered the intervention procedures. Thus, instead of earning points to exchange for tangible items or rewards, the teacher implemented a group reward condition in which children earned "honey" (i.e., cotton balls) to fill a "honey pot" (i.e., jar) for providing positive reports. The class earned a pizza party when the cotton balls filled the jar. Although peer ratings of the target student did not improve, positive interactions increased and negative interactions decreased. Furthermore, treatment acceptability ratings indicated that the teacher felt the intervention was effective, easy, and had future utility.

Classwide positive peer reporting: Tootling. During the PPR procedure, students are encouraged to focus their attention on a specific student's prosocial behavior. Another program developed by Skinner, Cashwell, and Skinner (2000) employs interdependent group contingencies to reinforce the entire class for reporting incidental prosocial behaviors of any classmate. Table 2 provides a brief description of tootling procedures. The tootling and PPR programs share some common procedures. With both procedures, brief group instruction is used to train students to report positive behaviors and reinforcement procedures are used to encourage students to report peers' incidental positive behavior.

There are several procedural differences between PPR and tootling. PPR targets specific children, often children who have been socially rejected. During tootling, all children are encouraged to monitor and report prosocial behaviors of *all classmates*. The behaviors targeted are also somewhat different. PPR targets general positive behavior while during tootling only reports of classmates actively helping peers are reinforced. During PPR, students publicly report target student positive behaviors. However, during tootling, students write reports of students helping students on index cards throughout the school day and turn them into the teacher at the end of the school day. Thus, reports of peers' positive behaviors are not made public. Finally, the tootling procedure employs an interdependent group contingency and feedback system similar to Ervin et al. (1996), where all tootles or reports of peers helping peers bring the class closer to earning a

Table 2
Step-by-Step Procedure for Tootling

1. Introduce and define tootling.

   Tootling is like tattling in that you report classmates' behavior. However, when tootling you only report when classmates help you or another classmate.

   Provide examples of classmates helping classmates and use group recitation to have students provide examples. Provide corrective feedback and reinforcement for responses.

   Teach students to write observations of peers helping peers on index cards taped to their desks. Specifically they write a) who, b) helped who, c) by_____ (here they write the prosocial behavior).

2. Explain the procedure.

   Each morning you will tape a blank index card to your desk. During the day you should record any instance you observe of peers helping peers.

   At the end of the school day, students turn in their index cards. If any student fills a card during the day they may turn it in and get another card.

   The teacher counts the number of tootles. Again only instances of peers helping peers are counted. Furthermore, if more than one student records the same instance, all count.

   The next morning the teacher announces how many tootles were recorded the previous day. The teacher adds the previous tootles and uses a group feedback chart to indicate cumulative tootles. Additionally, the teacher may read some examples of students helping students and praise the students.

   When the entire class reaches the cumulative tootle goal, the class earns a reinforcement (typically an activity).

3. After the group meets a goal the procedure is repeated with several possible alterations including:
   a. Change in the criteria to earn reinforcement as students become more skilled at tootling with practice.
   b. Change in the reinforcer. It may help for teachers to solicit reinforcers from students throughout the procedure. Additionally, using randomly selected group reinforcers is encouraged as some consequences may not be reinforcing for all students.

group reward. Despite several procedural and conceptual differences, both procedures are designed to structure the environment that enhances peer relationships.

Research on the tootling program has just begun. Two studies have been published where tootling procedures were implemented in general education second-grade (Cashwell et al., in press) and fourth-grade (Skinner et al., 2000) classrooms. These studies have shown that students can quickly learn to provide these written reports and the interdependent group contingency increases rates of tootling, while students report many incidental instances of prosocial behavior (e.g., a second-grade class provided 72 reports one day). Researchers continue to investigate the impact of tootling on students' social behaviors and perceptions of peers.

SUMMARY AND FUTURE RESEARCH

Students with behavior disorders may be more likely to be rejected by peers and receive fewer opportunities to interact with peers in unstructured social situations. Thus, these students may receive fewer opportunities to develop and master their social skills. PPR has been shown to increase both positive peer interaction rates and target students' initiation of social interactions, while decreasing negative peer interaction rates of socially rejected children (Jones et al., 2000; Robinson, 1998). Longitudinal research is needed to determine if these enhanced social interactions occasioned by PPR procedures provide neglected or rejected students with more opportunities to develop social skills within natural environments and whether these additional interactions can improve their social skills and their social status.

Although research on PPR and tootling is promising, there are several important limitations that should be addressed by future researchers. To date, PPR and tootling studies have shown that peer relations or peer reporting rates return to baseline levels when intervention is withdrawn. Although this pattern helps establish treatment effects, it also suggests that positive peer reporting and collateral effects (e.g., enhanced social status and social interactions) may not be maintained when these procedures are withdrawn. One potential reason that behaviors might return to baseline levels is the failure to address stimuli (both antecedent discriminative stimuli and reinforcing stimuli) for behaviors that compete with socially desirable behaviors (Gresham, 1998; Myerson & Hale, 1984). Thus, future researchers should determine if reducing reinforcement for socially inappropriate behavior in natural environments may enhance the impact of these programs. Also, researchers should determine if gradually fading PPR procedures enhances maintenance.

Research designed to describe and specify the causal mechanism responsible for positive outcomes should allow research to enhance these outcomes. It seems unlikely that a few praise statements each day could have much impact on social interactions if taunting, tattling, and intimidation continue at other times and in other settings. However, empirical data from the studies reviewed and anecdotal information from teachers (e.g., Jones et al., 2000) suggests that praise and tootling transfer to more natural contexts and reduce inappropriate peer interactions outside of the structured praise sessions. In order to more fully account for the behavioral processes responsible for improved peer relations, future researchers should determine what other specific social behaviors are occasioned in target students and peers by PPR by collecting data on social interactions during class, at breaks, or at recess (Ervin et al., 1996).

Understanding the causal mechanism(s) responsible for positive outcomes has applied implications. During the PPR program, peers provide *public* verbal praise to students with behavior disorders for their incidental prosocial behaviors. This public praise may cause students with behavior disorders to initiate more social interaction with children. Additionally, students who provided the verbal praise may be less likely to neglect or avoid the students who they praised. If outcomes are dependent upon the public praise statements, then one way to enhance these procedures may be to increase rates of public praise. Furthermore, if public praise is the causal mechanism, then children whose behavior is sensitive to peer attention may respond more favorably to positive peer reports. However, for other students (e.g., high-school students) public praise may be aversive stimuli (e.g., embarrassing stimuli). Therefore, public PPR may not be effective with these students.

It is possible that these PPR procedures are effective primarily because they increase peers' awareness of a rejected student's prosocial behavior. If this is the case, then outcomes may be enhanced through procedures designed to maximize students' awareness of all prosocial behaviors (e.g., tootling). Regardless, identifying the causal mechanism(s) responsible for the effectiveness of PPR procedures should enhance practitioners' ability to predict conditions (e.g., students, context, social environments) where PPR procedures are likely to be effective and strengthen these procedures in order to maximize their effectiveness.

Proactive punishment systems may be needed to prevent incidental antisocial behavior. The attention and energy placed into developing and implementing these systems may teach children that inappropriate behaviors are unacceptable, but do little to suggest that society values incidental nondramatic prosocial behaviors. Thus, future researchers should determine if implementing programs designed to encourage prosocial behaviors may help shape adults who value and respect incidental prosocial behaviors (Cashwell et al., in press).

Few simple yet effective strategies for promoting positive peer relations have been developed (Mather, Kavale, Quinn, Forness, & Rutherford, 1998). The current article describes research and theory that suggests that encouraging peers to monitor and report their classmates' incidental prosocial behaviors can enhance social relationships. The procedures described require little time as children quickly learn the steps in monitoring and reporting a peer's appropriate behavior. Furthermore, implementing these procedures within educational settings requires few additional resources. Thus, the strategies described in this article might also prove to be efficient and effective school-based prevention procedures (Sheridan & Gutkin, 2000). Given the heightened sensitivity in our culture to problems that may stem from peer isolation and rejection (e.g., school violence), future research should investigate whether schoolwide implementation of these or similar procedures may prove to be effective proactive strategies for promoting adaptive skills and enhancing peer relationships among all children.

REFERENCES

Algozzine, B. (1980). The disturbing child: A matter of opinion. Behavioral Disorders, 5, 112–115.

Asher, S.R., & Dodge, K.A. (1986). Identifying children who are rejected by their peers. Developmental Psychology, 22, 444–449.

Bandura, A. (1977). Social learning theory. Englewood Cliffs, NJ: Prentice-Hall.

Bierman, K.L., & Wargo, J.B. (1995). Predicting the longitudinal course associated with aggressive-rejected, aggressive (non-rejected), and rejected (nonaggressive) status. Development and Psychopathology, 7, 669–683.

Binder, C. (1996). Behavioral fluency: Evolution of a new paradigm. The Behavior Analyst, 19, 163–197

Boivin, M., Dodge, K.A., & Coie, J.D. (1995). Individual group behavioral similarity and peer status in experimental play groups of boys: The social misfit revisited. Journal of Personality and Social Psychology, 69, 269–279.

Bowers, F.E., McGinnis, C., Ervin, R.A., & Friman, P.C. (1999). Merging research and practice: The example of positive peer reporting applied to social rejection. Education and Treatment of Children, 22, 218–226.

Bowers, F.E., Woods, D.W., Carlyon, W.D., & Friman, P.C. (2000). Using positive peer reporting to improve the social interactions and acceptance of socially isolated adolescents in residential care: A systematic replication. Journal of Applied Behavior Analysis, 33, 239–242.

Bukowski, W.M., & Newcomb, A.F. (1984). Stability and determinants of sociometric status and friendship choice: A longitudinal perspective. Developmental Psychology, 20, 941–952.

Cashwell, T.H., Skinner, C.H., & Smith, E.S. (2001). Increasing second-grade students' reports of peers' prosocial behaviors via direct instruction, group reinforcement, and progress feedback: A replication and extension. Education and Treatment of Children, 24, 161–175.

Coie, J.D., & Cillessen, A.H. (1993). Peer rejection: Origins and effects on children's development. American Psychological Society, 2, 89–92.

Coie, J.D., & Dodge, K.A. (1983). Continuities and changes in children's social status: A five year longitudinal study. Merrill-Palmer Quarterly, 29, 261–282.

Coie, J.D., Dodge, K.A., & Kupersmidt, J.B. (1990). Peer group behavior and social status. In S.R. Asher & J.D. Coie (Eds.), Peer rejection in childhood (pp. 17–59). New York: Cambridge University Press.

Coie, J.D., Lochman, J., Terry, R., & Hyman, C. (1992). Predicting early adolescent disorder from childhood aggression and peer rejection. Journal of Consulting and Clinical Psychology, 60, 783–792.

Coie, J., Terry, R., Lenox, K., Lochman, J., & Hyman, C. (1995). Childhood peer rejection and aggression as predictors of stable patterns of adolescent disorder. Development and Psychopathology, 7, 697–713.

DeRosier, M.E., Kupersmidt, J.B., & Patterson, C.J. (1994). Children's academic and behavioral adjustment as a function of the chronicity and proximity of peer rejection. Child Development, 65, 1799–1813.

Dodge, K.A., Coie, J.D., Petit, G.S., & Price, J.M. (1990). Peer status and aggression in boys' groups: Developmental and contextual analyses. Child Development, 61, 1289–1301.

DuPaul, G.J., & Ekert, T. (1994). The effects of social skills curricula: Now you see them, now you don't. School Psychology Quarterly, 9, 113–132.

Ervin, R.A., Johnston, E.S., & Friman, P.C. (1998). Positive peer reporting to improve the social interactions of a socially rejected girl. Proven Practice: Prevention and Remediation Solutions for School Problems, 1, 17–21.

Ervin, R.A., Miller, P.M., & Friman, P.C. (1996). Feed the hungry bee: Using positive peer reports to improve the social interactions and acceptance of a socially rejected girl in a residential placement. Journal of Applied Behavior Analysis, 29, 251–253.

Forness, S.R., & Kavale, K.A. (1996). Treating social skill deficits in children with learning disabilities: A meta-analysis of the research. Learning Disabilities Quarterly, 19, 2–13.

Gresham, F.A. (1995). Best practices in social skills training. In A. Thomas & J. Grimes (Eds.), Best practices in school psychology–III (pp. 1021–1030). Washington, DC: The National Association of School Psychologists.

Gresham, F.A. (1998). Social skills training: Should we raze, remodel, or rebuild? Behavioral Disorders, 24, 19–25.

Grieger, T., Kaufman, J.M., & Grieger, R. (1976). Effects of peer reporting on cooperative play and aggression of kindergarten children. Journal of School Psychology, 14, 307–313.

Hall, R.V. (1991). Behavior analysis and education: An unfulfilled dream. Journal of Behavioral Education, 1, 305–316.

Haring, N.G., & Eaton, M.D. (1978). Systematic instructional procedures: An instructional hierarchy. In N.G. Haring, T.C. Lovitt, M.D. Eaton, & C.L. Hansen (Eds.), The fourth R: Research in the classroom (pp. 23–40). Columbus, OH: Merrill.

Hayes, L.A. (1976). The use of group contingencies for behavior control: A review. Psychological Bulletin, 83, 628–648.

Henington, C., & Skinner, C.H. (1998). Peer-monitoring. In K. Topping & S. Ehly (Eds.), Peer assisted learning (pp. 237–253). Hillsdale, NJ: Erlbaum.

Iwata, B.A., Dorsey, M.F., Slifer, K.J., Bauman, K.E., & Richman, G.S. (1994). Toward a functional analysis of self-injury. Journal of Applied Behavior Analysis, 27, 197–209.

Jones, K.M., Young, M.M., & Friman, P.C. (2000). Increasing peer praise of socially rejected delinquent youth: Effects on cooperation and acceptance. School Psychology Quarterly, 15, 30–39.

Kazdin, A.E. (2001). Behavior modification in applied settings (6th ed.). Belmont, CA: Wadsworth.

Ladd, G.W., Price, J.M., & Hart, C.H. (1990). Preschoolers' behavioral orientations and patterns of peer contact: Predictive of peer status? In S.R. Asher & J.D. Coie (Eds.), Peer rejection in childhood (pp. 90–115). New York: Cambridge University Press.

LaVigna, G.W., & Donnellan, A.M. (1986). Alternatives to punishment: Solving behavior problems with non-aversive strategies. New York: Irvington Publishers.

Litow, L., & Pumroy, D.K. (1975). A brief review of classroom group-oriented contingencies. Journal of Applied Behavior Analysis, 8, 341–347.

Mather, S.R., Kavale, K.A., Quinn, M.M., Forness, S.R., & Rutherford, R.B. (1998). Social skills interventions with students with emotional and behavioral problems: A quantitative synthesis of single-subject research. Behavioral Disorders, 23, 193–201.

McDowell, J.J. (1988). Matching theory in natural human environments. Behavior Analyst, 11, 95–109.

Myerson, J., & Hale, S. (1984). Practical implications of the matching law. Journal of Applied Behavior Analysis, 17, 367–380.

Newcomb, A.R., Bukowski, W.M., & Pattee, L. (1993). Children's peer relations: A meta-analytic review of popular, rejected, neglected, controversial, and average sociometric status. Psychological Bulletin, 113, 99–128.

Ogilvy, C.M. (1994). Social skills training with children and adolescents: A review of the evidence on effectiveness. Educational Psychology, 14, 73–83.

O'Leary, K.D., Poulos, R.W., & Devine, V.T. (1972). Tangible reinforcers: Bonuses or bribes. Journal of Consulting and Clinical Psychology, 38, 1–8.

Parker, J.G., & Asher, S.R. (1987). Peer relations and later personal adjustment: Are low-accepted children "at risk"? Psychological Bulletin, 102, 357–389.

Pumroy, D.K., & McIntire, R. (1991). Behavior analysis/modification for everyone. Journal of Behavioral Education, 1, 283–294.

Reisberg, L.E., Fudell, I., & Hudson, F. (1982). Comparison of responses to the behavior rating profile for mild to moderate behaviorally disordered subjects. Psychological Reports, 50, 136–138.

Robinson, S.L. (1998). Effects of positive statements made by peers on peer interactions and social status of children in a residential treatment setting. Unpublished doctoral dissertation, Mississippi State University, Starkville.

Sheridan, S.M., & Gutkin, T.B. (2000). The ecology of school psychology: Examining and changing our paradigm for the 21st century. School Psychology Review, 29, 485–502.

Skinner, C.H. (1998). Preventing academic skills deficits. In T.S. Watson & F. Gresham (Eds.), Handbook of child behavior therapy: Ecological considerations in assessment, treatment, and evaluation (pp. 61–83). New York: Plenum.

Skinner, C.H., Cashwell, T.H., & Skinner, A.L. (2000). Increasing tootling: The effects of a peer monitored group contingency program on students' reports of peers' prosocial behaviors. Psychology in the Schools, 37, 263–270.

Skinner, C.H., Skinner, C.F., Skinner, A.L., & Cashwell, T.C. (1999). Using interdependent group contingencies with groups of students: Why the principal kissed a pig at assembly. Educational Administration Quarterly, 35, 806–820.

Stormshak, E.A., Bierman, K.L., Bruschi, C., Dodge, K.A., Coie, J.D., & the Conduct Problems Prevention Research group. (1999). The relation between behavior problems and peer preference in different classroom contexts. Child Development, 70, 169–182.

Stumbo, N.J. (1995). Social skills instruction through commercially available resources. Therapeutic Recreation Journal, 29, 30–55.

Terry, R., & Coie, J.D. (1991). A comparison of methods for defining sociometric status among children. Developmental Psychology, 27, 867–880.

Thomas, J.D., Presland, I.E., Grant, M.D., & Glynn, T. (1978). Natural rates of teacher approval and disapproval in grade-7 classrooms. Journal of Applied Behavior Analysis, 11, 91–94.

White, M.A. (1975). Natural rates of teacher approval and disapproval in the classroom. Journal of Applied Behavior Analysis, 8, 367–372.

Wielkiewicz, R.M. (1995). Behavior management in the schools: Principles and procedures (2nd ed.). Boston: Allyn and Bacon.

Winette, R.A., & Winkler, R.C. (1972). Current behavior modification in the classroom: Be quiet, be docile. Journal of Applied Behavior Analysis, 5, 499–504.

Wright, J.C., Giammarino, M., & Parad, H.W. (1986). Social status in small groups: Individual-group similarity and the social "misfit." Journal of Personality and Social Psychology, 50, 523–536.

Psychology in the Schools, Vol. 39(2), 2002
© 2002 Wiley Periodicals, Inc.

DOI: 10.1002/pits.10031

SELF-MODELING AS AN EFFECTIVE INTERVENTION FOR STUDENTS WITH SERIOUS EMOTIONAL DISTURBANCE: ARE WE MODIFYING CHILDREN'S MEMORIES?

THOMAS J. KEHLE, MELISSA A. BRAY, SUZANNE G. MARGIANO, AND LEA A. THEODORE

University of Connecticut

ZHENG ZHOU

St. John's University

The intent of this article is to consider similarities between the research on the alteration of memory, and that on the modification of behavior through viewing edited self-modeling videotapes that depict exemplary behavior. A considerable number of studies unequivocally show that memory can be altered through several mechanisms, including visual techniques. However, there is limited research indicating that alteration of memory results in valued and adaptive behavioral change. This article explores a tenable explanation for the research finding that self-modeling is an effective intervention for students with behavior disorders. It was hypothesized that when participants view a change in their behavior, their memories and self-beliefs subsequently change to be in concert with that shown on the edited videotape. Perhaps as the individuals repeatedly view the videotapes, they alter their memory of engagement in past maladaptive behavior, with an adaptive memory of exemplary behavior. Further, they may come to believe that they were always capable of exhibiting such behavior. © 2002 Wiley Periodicals, Inc.

The purpose of this article is to present a novel explanation for effectiveness of the self-modeling intervention with students with serious emotional disturbance (SED). The brief overview of self-modeling and behavior disorders will be followed by the argument that alteration of the student's memory may be the causal mechanism that allows behavior change.

Self-modeling has been defined as "an intervention procedure using the observation of images of oneself engaged in adaptive behavior. Most commonly, these images are captured on video, edited into 2–4 minute vignettes, and repeatedly reviewed to learn skills or adjust to challenging environments as part of a training or therapy protocol" (Dowrick, 1999, p. 23). The procedure, in comparison to other interventions or therapies, is relatively nonintrusive in that it requires very little of the individual's time. Typically, the brief videotapes are shown on 6 to 8 occasions over a period of 4 to 6 weeks (Bray & Kehle, 2001). Substantial empirical support has been noted for the effectiveness of self-modeling in that over 150 studies successfully dealing with a myriad of behaviors have been published to date in the professional literature (Dowrick, 1999).

The effectiveness of self-modeling has most often been explained in terms of Bandura's social cognitive theory (1986). Social cognitive theory postulates that behavior change is mediated by self-efficacy. For example, Kehle, Owen, and Cressy (1990) used self-modeling to effect a complete cessation of selective mutism in a 6-year-old student. It was hypothesized that the child with selective mutism possessed adequate verbal skills but lacked the self-efficacy to employ those skills in the school setting. Kehle et al. further theorized that the child, through viewing his self-modeled verbal behavior (i.e., edited videotapes that depicted him talking in his classroom), altered his self-efficacious beliefs. Specifically, he believed he could successfully converse with his classmates and teacher because his efficacious beliefs were modified to be in concert with those verbal behaviors depicted on the intervention videotape.

Dowrick (1999) proposed a parsimonious explanation of the positive change in behavior that results from repeated viewings of oneself on edited videotapes by simply stating that "the obser-

---

Correspondence to: Thomas Kehle, PhD, Department of Educational Psychology, U-2064, University of Connecticut, Storrs, CT 06269. E-mail: kehle@uconn.edu

vation of one's adaptative or valued behavior increases the future likelihood of that behavior" (p. 36). This proposal, as he stated, is fundamental to Bandura's (1986) social cognitive theory. Dowrick further stated that although the learning that takes place as a consequence of observing one's behavior is compatible with social cognitive theory and is consistent with the theoretical bases of operant and classical conditioning, it nevertheless should be considered a "learning mechanism in its own right, not a special case of observational learning from others with some positive reinforcement, reciprocal inhibition, cognitive restructuring, and self-efficacy added in" (p. 36).

Dowrick (1999) suggested that self-modeling could be classified into seven major applications, including increasing adaptive behavior (e.g., reducing disruptive classroom behavior by increasing on-task behavior), transfer of behavior across settings (e.g., selective mutism), support for anxiety- and mood-based disorders, recombining component skills (e.g., a triple lutz in figure skating), transference of role play (e.g., personal safety training), and engagement in a low-frequency skill (e.g., physical exercise). Furthermore, these seven applications can be broadly conceptualized as positive self-review, feedforward, or a combination of both. In positive self-review, the attempt is to maximize the performance of a target skill. That is, it is a reconstruction of "an achieved, exemplary behavior, presumably in need of strengthening" (Dowrick, 1999, p. 26). Conversely, feedforward involves editing the videotape to exclude inappropriate behavior in order to construct images of the individual's best possible adaptive behaviors. "Feedfoward constructs a previously unachieved, but possible future, or target, behavior" (Dowrick, 1999, p. 26). It is assumed that there is greater probability for change if the behavior has not yet previously occurred, and therefore, feedforward yields far greater changes in behavior than positive self-review (Dowrick, 1999). Dowrick's summation suggested considerable value in capitalizing on the learning that presumably occurs as a consequence of viewing images of one's future behavior.

The intent of this paper is to present an alternative argument for why self-modeling is effective, particularly with respect to students with SED. Specifically, we suggest that the behavior change brought about as a consequence of self-modeling is mediated by changing the individual's memory of the performance, or nonperformance, of the target behavior.

Students with SED exhibit problematic behaviors that cannot be attributed to intellectual, sensory, or physical deficits. These behaviors are "persistent and are of sufficient severity and deviancy from age and/or social norms that they substantially interfere with the learning process, mediate against satisfactory interpersonal relationships, and impair the academic and social functioning of themselves and, perhaps others" (Kehle, Bray, Theodore, Jenson, & Clark, 2000; p. 475). Specifically, these students are characteristically noncompliant, inattentive, and disruptive. Inordinate amounts of teacher time are taken from academic tasks and reallocated to address these behavior problems (Kehle et al., 2000).

Addressing students who evidence disruptive classroom behavior is often a tedious, frustrating, and unsuccessful experience. Those interventions that appear effective typically involve considerable intrusion on instructional time. However, perhaps the least intrusive intervention may arguably be self-modeling in that it requires minimal treatment time.

Kehle, Clark, Jenson, and Wampold (1986) employed an ABA withdrawal design, replicated three times, plus a control and a follow-up phase to examine the effects of self-modeling. The four male participants with SED, aged 10 to 13 years, were placed in a self-contained classroom that included eight other students with SED. The criteria for disruptive classroom behavior were defined according to O'Leary, Romanzcyk, Kass, Dietz, and Santogrossi (1979) and included the occurrence of any of the following: touching, vocalizing, aggression, playing, disorientating, making noise, and out of seat. Kehle et al. videotaped approximately 25 minutes of each student's classroom behavior. Subsequently, the tapes were edited to remove all instances of the above seven behaviors. This resulted in 12-minute-long intervention videotapes that depicted relatively exemplary behavior. The intervention tapes were shown back to the students on five or six occasions over a 2-week period of time. The treatment effect was substantial in that the intervals of disruptive behaviors were reduced from a baseline average of 47% to 11% after a 6-week follow-up.

Clare, Jenson, Kehle, and Bray (2000) found similar positive effects in a study that employed a multiple baseline design across three students. Classroom peers' on-task behavior was used as comparison data. The results indicated "immediate, substantial, and durable changes in students' on-task behavior that generalized across academic settings. The three students evidenced an increase of on-task behavior from an average of 33% of the intervals observed at baseline to 86% during treatment. At a 6- and 8-week follow-up, the students' percentages of on-task behavior were essentially indistinguishable from their classroom peers" (Clare et al., 2000; p. 517). In addition, consumer data indicated that both teachers and students were quite satisfied with the procedure.

Further, Dowrick and Raeburn (1977), Shear and Shapiro (1993), Walker and Clement (1992), and Woltersdorf (1992) all found that the self-modeling procedure substantially reduced inappropriate classroom behavior with concomitant increases in on-task behavior. In addition, although less pronounced, McCurdy and Shapiro (1988) and Possell, Kehle, McLoughlin, and Bray (1999) reported idiosyncratic results with similar participants.

As Dowrick (1999) has argued, these dramatic results can be explained as a form of learning that involves the observation of one's adaptive or valued behavior, and that through self-observation, the probability of the future occurrence of that behavior is increased. However, a plausible alternative, and perhaps more comprehensive explanation, is that repeated observations of oneself engaged in either valued or *not valued behavior* may alter the individual's memory of whether or not s/he previously performed that behavior. Moreover, this distortion of memory may function to increase the probability of the future occurrence of that behavior.

The history of research on memory has indicated that it is dynamic, fluid, and alterable (Loftus, 1997). The concept of memory distortion, or the process of altering memories of actual events, has been demonstrated in several investigations (Schacter, 1995). Further, according to Loftus (1997), it is relatively easy to "create complex and elaborate false memories in the minds of research subjects, and that subjects are confident that these false memories are real" (p. 61). The proposed mechanisms involved included strong external suggestion, pressure to remember more, and encouragement to simply imagine past false memories (Loftus, 1997). Also, Schacter (1999) noted that memory can be altered in several ways including bias (contemporary events influence remembering the past), persistence of traumatic memories, misattribution (falsely attributing the source of a memory), and suggestibility (outside influence on one's memory).

The potential relationship between this memory research and the effectiveness of self-modeling is compelling, particularly when considering the research dealing with misattribution and suggestibility. Similar to the simple technique of inducing images of events that never took place to create a false memory (Loftus, 1997), individuals when viewing the edited self-modeling videotapes may create a false memory that they have previously, or can subsequently, successfully replicate the visually depicted behavior. Again, as previously discussed, this notion is consistent with social cognitive theory to the extent that behavior change is mediated by the alteration of memory that one can successfully engage in that behavior, or, in other words, that one's efficacious beliefs are altered. Efficacious beliefs may be modified to the extent that they become in concert with those behaviors depicted on the self-modeling intervention videotape. This is consistent with the notion that behavior precedes beliefs, particularly at the point of altering behavior. Subsequently, the change in self-beliefs and behavior becomes circuitous, in effect influencing each other.

It appears that visual information is more powerful than verbal information in altering memories (Braun & Loftus, 1998). Further, after the memory is altered through visual techniques, it is relatively resistant to change, even when verbal arguments are presented to discredit the memory (Braun & Loftus). Apparently, individuals who are exposed to visual misinformation, come to "really believe in the veracity and strength of the newly created memories, and they report visually re-experiencing the information" (p. 577). In addition, and perhaps more importantly, Braun and Loftus found that altering memories can result in a change in behavior. Specifically, in their investigation on the effects of misinformation in advertising, they showed that "memory changes can be directly linked to consumer subjective judgements and choices when the misinformation is particularly salient" (p. 569). Obviously, the use of edited videotapes depicting a target behavior would maximize salience. The following quote taken from Braun and Loftus is relevant to our argument:

> Advertising is far from important or harmless; it is not a mere mirror image. Its power is real, and on the brink of a great increase. Not the power to brainwash overnight, but the power to create subtle and real change. The power to prevail. (As cited in Clark, 1985)

However, we believe that the expected effect of presenting edited videotapes to students that depict them engaged in exemplary behavior would not only mimic the effects realized in visually conveyed advertising, but would exceed it. In self-modeling, the effect is enhanced in that student identification and similarity with the model are maximized. Further, multiple viewings of the intervention videotapes over several weeks capitalize on the spacing effect, which refers to the research finding that spaced or distributed presentations of information, in comparison to a single massed presentation, result in substantially better learning (Dempster, 1988).

DISCUSSION

The intent of this article has been to explore the possible relationship between memory alteration and the effects of videotaped self-modeling as an intervention. It has been shown that visual techniques can lead to altered memories and subsequently to behavior change (Braun & Loftus, 1998). Therefore, it is plausible that a visual technique such as self-modeling is operating similarly. Perhaps participants who view edited self-modeling videotapes that depict exemplary behavior change their behavior and their self-beliefs to be in concert with the behavior depicted on the videotape. Specifically, students with SED who repeatedly view edited videotapes of themselves engaged in appropriate classroom behavior may supplant their memory of their past maladaptive with exemplary behavior. They believe that they are not only capable of performing these exemplary behaviors in actual day-to-day classroom activities, but that they were historically capable of such behavior.

Perhaps the next logical step is to conduct experimental investigations to address this hypothesis. The potential finding that self-modeling leads to memory alteration would prove useful in the design of psychological interventions.

REFERENCES

Bandura, A. (1986). Social foundations of thought and action: A social-cognitive theory. Englewood Cliffs, NJ: Prentice-Hall.

Braun, K.A., & Loftus, E.F. (1998). Advertising's misinformation effect. Applied Cognitive Psychology, 12, 569–591.

Bray, M.A., & Kehle, T.J. (2001). Long-term effects of self-modeling as an intervention for stuttering. School Psychology Review, 30, 131–137.

Clare, S.K., Jenson, W.R., Kehle, T.J., & Bray, M.A. (2000). Self-modeling as a treatment for increasing on-task behavior. Psychology in the Schools, 37, 517–522.

Clark, E. (1985). The want makers: Inside the world of advertising. New York: Penguin Books.

Dempster, F.N. (1988). The spacing effect: A case study in the failure to apply the results of psychological research. American Psychologist, 43, 627–634.

Dowrick, P.W. (1999). A review of self modeling and related interventions. Applied and Preventive Psychology, 8, 23–39.

Dowrick, P.W., & Raeburn, J.M. (1977). Video editing and medication to produce a therapeutic self model. Journal of Consulting and Clinical Psychology, 45, 1156–1158.

Kehle, T.J., Bray, M.A., Theodore, L.A., Jenson, W.R., & Clark, E. (2000). A multi-component intervention designed to reduce disruptive classroom behavior. Psychology in the Schools, 37, 475–481.

Kehle, T.J., Clark, E., Jenson, W.R., & Wampold, B.E. (1986). Effectiveness of self-observation with behavior disordered elementary school children. School Psychology Review, 15, 289–295.

Kehle, T.J., Owen, S.V., & Cressy, E.T. (1990). The use of self-modeling as an intervention in school psychology: A case study of an elective mute. School Psychology Review, 19, 115–121.

Loftus, E.F. (1997). Memories for a past that never was. Current Directions in Psychological Science, 6, 60–65.

McCurdy, B.L., & Shapiro, E.S. (1988). Self-observation and the reduction of inappropriate classroom behavior. Journal of School Psychology, 26, 371–378.

O'Leary, K.D., Romanzcyk, R.G., Kass, R.E., Dietz, A., & Santogrossi, D. (1979). Procedures for classroom observation of teachers and children. Unpublished manuscript, State University of New York at Stony Brook, Stony Brook, New York.

Possell, L.E., Kehle, T.J., McLoughlin, C.S., & Bray, M.A. (1999). Self-modeling as an intervention to reduce inappropriate classroom behavior. Cognitive and Behavioral Practice, 6, 99–105.

Schacter, D.L. (1995). Memory distortion: How minds, brains, and societies reconstruct the past. Cambridge, MA.: Harvard University Press.

Schacter, D.L. (1999). The seven sins of memory: Insights from psychology and cognitive neuroscience. American Psychologist, 54, 182–203.

Shear, S.M., & Shapiro, E.S. (1993). Effects of using self-recording and self-observation in reducing disruptive behavior. Journal of School Psychology, 31, 519–534.

Walker, C.J., & Clement, P.W. (1992). Treating inattentive, impulsive, hyperactive children with self-modeling and stress inoculation training. Child and Family Behavior Therapy, 14, 164–171.

Woltersdorf, M.A. (1992). Videotape self-modeling in the treatment of attention-deficit hyperactivity disorder. Child and Family Behavior Therapy, 14, 53–73.

Psychology in the Schools, Vol. 39(2), 2002
© 2002 Wiley Periodicals, Inc.

DOI: 10.1002/pits.10032

NEGATIVE TREATMENT OUTCOMES OF BEHAVIORAL PARENT TRAINING PROGRAMS

AMY E. ASSEMANY

State University of New York at Albany

DAVID E. McINTOSH

Ball State University

The purposes of this review were to: (a) outline the literature on negative treatment outcomes of behavioral parent training programs, (b) detail variables found to be predictive of negative treatment outcomes, and (c) suggest future directions of study. We suggest that despite scores of studies documenting positive outcomes of behavioral parent training programs, negative treatment outcomes occur for a sizeable minority of families. Existing research has documented a relationship between a number of contextual stressors and negative outcomes. More research is necessary before the knowledge of the current literature can be applied to clinical practice. Suggestions for needed research are given, including determining which contextual life stressors play a critical role in the relationship, assessing the effect of contextual stressors on various treatments, and determining how contextual life stressors impact the treatment process. © 2002 Wiley Periodicals, Inc.

The positive outcomes of behavioral parent training (BPT) programs have been well documented and provide justification for these treatments to be considered "best practice" or "empirically supported" for most populations (Lonigan, Elbert, & Johnson, 1998). Yet, valuable information can be gained about the effectiveness of behavioral parent training programs by examining the circumstances and mechanisms involved in negative treatment outcomes or the "treatment failures" (Kazdin, Holland, Crowley, & Breton, 1997). Unfortunately, these negative outcomes have not received as much attention in the literature as the positive treatment outcomes of behavioral parent training programs (Stoiber & Kratochwill, 2000). The present review has three purposes: (a) to define and outline the literature on negative treatment outcomes of behavioral parent training programs, (b) to examine the literature on variables predictive of negative treatment outcomes, and (c) to suggest future directions of study in the hope of improving treatments to the sizeable minority of families who experience negative treatment outcomes.

BEHAVIORAL PARENT TRAINING PROGRAMS

Behavioral parent training (BPT) programs are often recommended for preschool children exhibiting a clinical level of disruptive behaviors and their parents (Kazdin, 1997). The disruptive behaviors targeted by the treatment often include temper tantrums, noncompliance, aggression, defiance, stealing, and destruction of property (McMahon & Wells, 1998). If untreated, the conduct problems exhibited by children often become increasingly debilitating over time (Campbell, 1994). Children who do not receive or respond favorably to treatment are at risk of developing a wide range of problems later in life, such as interpersonal problems, juvenile delinquency, poor school performance, school dropout, substance abuse, adult crime, and antisocial personality disorder (Kazdin, 1995). A number of BPT programs have been supported steadily by efficacy studies describing the outcomes for families that complete the treatment (Lonigan et al., 1998). Examples of such BPT programs are the Living with Children Program (Patterson, Reid, Jones, & Conger,

This manuscript in an abbreviated version of the first author's chapter two of her dissertation that was submitted in partial fulfillment of the requirements for the degree of Doctor of Psychology in the School Psychology Program at the State University of New York at Albany.

Correspondence to: Amy Assemany, 42798 Lilley Pointe, Canton, MI 48187. E-mail: demcintosh@bsu.edu

1975), a group discussion/videotape modeling program (Webster-Stratton, 1981b), Parent-Child Interaction Therapy (PCIT; Eyberg & Robinson, 1982), the Helping the Noncompliant Child program (Forehand & McMahon, 1981), and the Delinquency Prevention program (Tremblay et al., 1992). These programs share similar treatment goals, procedures, underlying assumptions, and outcomes. Each of these programs have been identified by the Task Force on Effective Psychosocial Interventions initiated by Division 12 of the American Psychological Association as either "empirically supported" or "probably efficacious"(Lonigan, Elbert, & Johnson, 1998).

In general, empirically supported BPT programs have demonstrated short-term and long-term efficacy for the majority of families who completed the training (Brestan & Eyberg, 1998). The short-term effects include improvement in the target child's behaviors, such as increased compliance to parent's directives, and decreased oppositional and aggressive behaviors; along with enhanced parenting skills in the form of parents spending more time attending to and rewarding their child's positive behaviors, and giving better, more appropriate commands, warnings, and discipline (Eyberg & Robinson, 1982; Henry, 1985; Webster-Stratton, 1982; Wiltz & Patterson, 1974). When short-term effects have occurred as a result of BPT, they often have generalized to settings other than an outpatient clinic, the typical location of service delivery. For example, for many families decreased disruptive behaviors have been documented in the home (Eisenstadt, Eyberg, McNeil, Newcomb, & Funderburk, 1993; Forehand, Rogers, Steffe, & Middlebrook, 1984; Peed, Roberts, & Forehand, 1977; Webster-Stratton, 1984), school (Forehand, Breiner, McMahon, & Davies, 1981; McNeil, Eyberg, Eisenstadt, Newcomb, & Funderburk, 1991), and community settings (Webster-Stratton, 1998).

Support of the long-term effects of BPT for some families who complete the treatment has been documented in the literature (Long, Forehand, Wierson, & Morgan, 1994). Due to the difficulties inherent in longitudinal research, limited data exist to support the long-term effects of BPT (Kazdin, 1997). Nevertheless, the existing studies suggest reductions in clinically significant disruptive behaviors for many children assessed 1 to 2 years after completing PCIT (Eyberg & Boggs, 1998), and sustained improvements in parenting skills for many parents who successfully completed treatment (Eyberg & Boggs, 1998; Forehand & Long, 1988; Long et al., 1994; Webster-Stratton, 1982, 1990b; Webster-Stratton & Hammond, 1997).

NEGATIVE TREATMENT OUTCOMES OF BEHAVIORAL PARENT TRAINING

Despite the scores of outcome studies demonstrating the numerous benefits of BPT programs for the treatment of young children with conduct problems and their parents, a consistent mention of negative outcomes of BPT programs also exists in the literature for a sizeable minority of families (Cataldo, 1984; Eyberg & Boggs, 1998; Forehand, Middlebrook, Rogers, & Steffe, 1983; Prinz & Miller, 1994; Serketich & Dumas, 1996; Webster-Stratton & Hammond, 1997). Three types of negative treatment outcomes occur in BPT programs and have been examined to date. They are: (1) high rates of premature family dropout, (2) failure of parents to engage and truly participate in treatment throughout the process, and (3) failure of the parents and child to maintain positive changes made in treatment at follow-up (Miller & Prinz, 1990). The high rate of sporadic participation, premature dropout, and behavioral outcomes remaining in the clinical range for a considerable number of families present a major obstacle to successful BPT (Serketich & Dumas, 1996), limiting the effectiveness of these "empirically supported" treatments with particular families.

The study of negative treatment outcomes has received less attention in the literature than the documentation of positive outcomes (Prinz & Miller, 1994). This relative oversight of the topic of negative treatment outcomes resulted primarily from two factors: excitement about the promise of BPT programs after many positive effects were observed for families who engaged fully in the treatment, and lack of publication of studies not demonstrating positive results or statistically significant effects. Behavioral parent training programs offered psychologists working with families of children with conduct problems one of the first effective treatments available for this population (Kazdin, 1987). As a result, it is not surprising that the vast amount of scholarly writing in this area focused strictly on the benefits and promise of the treatment, and not on the negative treatment outcomes occurring for a sizable minority of families who participated (Forehand et al., 1983). Coupled with the reporting of exciting, positive findings, the tradition of journals to publish only studies with statistically significant effects leads to an underrepresentation of literature about the negative outcomes of treatment (Stoiber & Kratochwill, 2000). Stoiber and Kratochwill argue that negative results of empirically supported interventions offer valuable information to the field in that a pattern of negative results is likely indicative of particular conditions under which a treatment is not effective. Without the reporting and examination of information about families who are not satisfied or helped by BPT programs, the effectiveness of this treatment for this population may not improve.

Premature Termination

The first negative treatment outcome, high rates of premature family dropout, appears to be the most studied out of the three types of negative outcomes discussed in the BPT literature. A literature review conducted by Forehand et al. (1983) discovered that out of 45 parent training studies published in eight popular journals between 1972 and 1982, only 22 (49%) studies contained dropout data. This data indicated that the reported dropout rate in parent training in those years was 28%. Consistent with the 49% rate of reporting dropout data in parent training outcome studies, published reports of the five BPT programs with the most empirical support have not always included the number of families who prematurely dropped out of training (Bernal, Klinnert, & Schultz, 1980; Brestan, Eyberg, Boggs, & Algina, 1997; Eyberg & Robinson, 1982; Forehand et al., 1983; Tremblay, Pagani-Kurtz, Masse, Vitaro, & Phil, 1995). These efficacy studies frequently report the positive outcomes of the treatment, yet do not specify that these outcomes only occurred for families who completed treatment. No information is available about those families not completing treatment, other than the fact that they received no treatment at the time of the study.

When treatment dropout rates have been documented in reports of BPT programs, the data have varied. Reported dropout rates range from 8–48% (Eisenstadt et al., 1993; Eyberg & Johnson, 1974; Kazdin, Holland, & Crowley, 1997; McMahon, Forehand, & Griest, 1981; Prinz & Miller, 1994; Webster-Stratton, 1981a, 1993, 1994). Notably, reports of treatment dropout rates have been the lowest when Webster-Stratton's (1981a, 1994) BPT program has been used. The high rate of premature termination has a number of ramifications, including the fact that families who drop out are less likely to improve compared to families who complete treatment, families with significant impairment remain untreated, and costs for the provision of clinical services for all families frequently increase (Kazdin, Mazurick, & Siegel, 1994; Kazdin, Holland & Crowley, 1997; Prinz & Miller, 1994). Overall, data on BPT treatment dropout rates suggest that a sizable number of families qualified to receive BPT do not complete the treatment, and therefore do not benefit from the therapeutic gains observed in most families who complete these "empirically supported" treatments.

Poor Treatment Engagement

The second negative treatment outcome discussed in the literature, failure of the parents to engage and truly participate in treatment throughout the process, has not received much mention in the literature on BPT programs (Miller & Prinz, 1990). Specific parental behaviors that have been defined as insufficient treatment engagement include inadequate treatment session participation (e.g., refusing to participate in role plays or discussions), dissatisfaction with the treatment regimen (e.g., hostile interactions when the therapist makes suggestions), sporadic attendance, and noncompliance (e.g., not completing homework assignments); these behaviors have been also referred to as resistance in the literature (Chamberlain & Baldwin, 1987; Jahn & Lichstein, 1980; Miller & Prinz, 1990). Although insufficient data exists about treatment outcomes specific to parents who resist BPT or do not fully participate in treatment, it is likely that resistive parental behaviors compromise the potential positive effects of full participation in BPT programs.

Lack of Maintained Progress

The third negative treatment outcome, failure of the parents and child to maintain positive changes made in treatment at follow-up, refers to both the lack of maintenance of skills at post-treatment assessment, and the assessment of the child's behavior to have returned to a clinical level of impairment at posttreatment (Miller & Prinz, 1990). Despite favorable results upon completion of a BPT program, researchers have begun to acknowledge the limited benefit of those treatment gains if the child's overall adjustment at the follow-up assessment was not maintained in the normal or nonclinical range of functioning (Jacobsen, Follette, & Revenstorf, 1984; Webster-Stratton, 1990b). Serketich and Dumas (1996) commented after conducting a meta-analysis that only a small percentage of available BPT outcome studies were methodologically rigorous enough to allow for an analysis of the clinical utility of BPT at follow-up. In other words, very few studies examined whether the impact of treatment continued to make a difference in everyday functioning over time by conducting a follow-up comparison of experimental and control groups with clinically sensitive measures. When clinical significance has been examined, long-term follow-up studies suggest that 30–40% of parents who participate in treatment rate their child's behavior in the clinical range at the time of follow-up assessment (Forehand, Furey, & McMahon, 1984; Webster-Stratton, 1990a, 1990b). This finding indicates that after the completion of treatment, the functioning of many of the children treated continued to measure in the clinical range.

Summary

Behavioral parent training programs have a relatively long history of success in the treatment of most young children with conduct problems and their families. Successful completion of BPT programs has led to numerous short-term and long-term positive outcomes (Kazdin, 1997). Although less studied, a sizeable minority of families do not benefit from BPT programs and instead experience negative treatment outcomes. Included under the umbrella of negative treatment outcomes is a family who prematurely drops out of treatment, does not engage in the process of treatment, or does not demonstrate positive gains following BPT. Historically, families who have not completed the prescribed treatment have not been described in published outcome studies (Prinz & Miller, 1994), nor has research finding negative treatment results been published by major journals (Stoiber & Kratochwill, 2000). However, the relatively small number of studies focused on this population provides valuable information about characteristics that appear shared among families at-risk for experiencing negative treatment outcomes. This literature suggests that despite being "empirically supported" for most participants, not all families in need of BPT are benefiting at this time from such treatment.

CONTEXTUAL VARIABLES PREDICTIVE OF NEGATIVE TREATMENT OUTCOMES

As a result of studies describing the negative outcomes of BPT, researchers began to document child, parent, and family characteristics associated with negative treatment outcomes (Serketich & Dumas, 1996). In the literature, these characteristics are also commonly referred to as contextual variables impacting treatment outcome. To identify variables predictive of negative treatment outcomes researchers have used primarily two types of analyses: post hoc and descriptive methods (Serketich & Dumas, 1996). Most often in BPT efficacy studies, demographic information and pretreatment measures used to quantify problematic behaviors are collected at intake, prior to the commencement of the treatment. This information is later used to describe the characteristics of those families not demonstrating favorable outcomes as measured by the study or those prematurely dropping out of treatment. In some cases, researchers also have conducted post hoc analyses with this information after the implementation of the BPT program to determine child, parent, and family characteristics statistically associated with the families who did not engage in the treatment process, dropped out prematurely, or did not demonstrate positive outcomes.

The BPT literature on contextual variables associated with negative treatment outcomes indicates three consistently mentioned characteristics predictive of poor outcomes: socioeconomic disadvantage, family dysfunction, and severity of the child's externalizing behaviors (Bernal, 1984; Eyberg, Boggs, & Rodriguez, 1992; Kazdin, 1987; Kazdin & Wassell, 1999; McMahon & Forehand, 1984; Prinz & Miller, 1996; Webster-Stratton, 1985, 1990c). The first two of these characteristics include in each category a number of related variables that appear associated with each other, yet fall under the broad category of either socioeconomic disadvantage or family dysfunction. The following review of the literature on contextual variables will detail the three characteristics suggested by research to be predictive of poor outcomes.

Socioeconomic Disadvantage

The powerful association between socioeconomic disadvantage and negative treatment outcomes has been demonstrated repeatedly in the literature (Kazdin, 1997; Serketich & Dumas, 1996). Since the early 1980s, BPT researchers have associated poor treatment outcomes or premature treatment termination with families of low socioeconomic status (Dumas & Wahler, 1983; Wahler, 1980). Dumas and Wahler, publishing in the early 1980s, defined socioeconomic disadvantage as the presence of at least four out of six risk variables. The risk variables comprising their Socioeconomic Disadvantage Index were family income (below $13,000), maternal education (no college education), family composition (one-parent household), family size (three or more children), source of referral (social agency referral), and area of residence (high crime neighborhood). These six risk variables defined the variable socioeconomic disadvantage in the early 1980s.

From the mid-1980s to the mid-1990s, criteria used to define socioeconomic disadvantage in the literature began to expand. A few additional risk variables were added to the definition of socioeconomic disadvantage, namely, ethnicity (minority status), type of insurance (Medicaid), inadequate housing, and unemployment (Armbruster & Fallon, 1994; Dumas & Wahler, 1983). Moreover, during this time, researchers began to suggest specific variables underlying the influence of the broad characteristic of socioeconomic disadvantage. For example, ordinary daily inconveniences experienced by those who are socioeconomically disadvantaged, such as inflexible and demanding work schedules, a lack of child care coverage, and unreliable transportation, were suggested as variables subsumed under the broad category of socioeconomic disadvantage that may be adversely impacting treatment participation (Prinz & Miller, 1996). Thus, with time, scholars have acknowledged the complexity of the variable socioeconomic disadvantage and broadened the variables included in the definition of the term.

The more recent BPT outcome studies, conducted in the latter half of the 1990s, continued to expand the definition of socioeconomic disadvantage. Some studies during this time hinted at the interconnectedness of contextual variables by making reference to "socioeconomic disadvantage and related family conditions" and the "adverse effect of poverty and its accompanying stressors" (Kazdin & Wassell, 1999; Webster-Stratton, 1990c). Included in the definition of socioeconomic disadvantage were variables such as the educational and occupational attainment of the family,

family income, receipt of public assistance, mother's age, family structure, minority group membership, and type of insurance (Forehand & Kotchick, 1996; Kazdin & Wassell, 1999; Webster-Stratton, 1990c).

Evident from the review of outcome studies reporting the association between socioeconomic disadvantage and negative BPT treatment outcomes, the criteria used to define the variable has changed over time. As more research is conducted in this area, the trend appears to be the inclusion of more variables under the broad category of socioeconomic disadvantage (Kazdin & Wassell, 1999). At different times in the BPT literature, all of the following variables have been included in various definitions of socioeconomic disadvantage: family income, maternal education, family composition, family size, source of referral, and area of residence, ethnicity, type of insurance, occupational attainment of the parent(s), mother's age, inflexible and demanding work schedules, a lack of child care coverage, and unreliable transportation (Armbruster & Fallon, 1994; Dumas & Albin, 1986; Dumas & Wahler, 1983; Forehand & Kotchick, 1996; Kazdin & Wassell, 1999; Prinz & Miller, 1996). The number of variables used to define this family characteristic in and of itself indicates the broadness of the category of one's socioeconomic situation; subsumed under this category are many variables, some directly a result of poverty and others considered associated stressors.

Family Dysfunction

The second category of family characteristics predictive of negative treatment outcomes is family dysfunction. This variable has also been identified since at least the early 1980s as predictive of poor BPT outcomes or premature termination from BPT. Earlier research identified variables such as mother insularity (Dumas & Wahler, 1983; Wahler, 1980), maternal depression (Griest, Forehand, & Wells, 1981), the presence of the father, marital violence, and maternal psychopathology (Dumas, 1984) to be driving the association between family dysfunction and negative treatment outcomes. The term, "mother insularity," first described by Wahler, Leske, and Rogers (1979) refers to mothers who have few and/or aversive day-to-day social contacts. Moreover, the limited social contacts are not with friends, but most often with family or social service agents, and are usually not initiated by the mothers. These parental-interactional variables were considered the influences accounting for the association between family dysfunction and negative BPT outcomes. Maternal psychopathology typically was defined as the mother's reported history of psychological/psychiatric symptoms or disorder for which she had sought professional help at least once since the child's birth.

Behavioral parent training outcome studies conducted between the mid-1980s and mid-1990s continued to include variables such as parental psychopathology, especially maternal depression, father's presence, insularity, and marital violence under the umbrella category of family dysfunction (Dumas & Albin, 1986; Gould, Shaffer, & Kaplan, 1985). However, similar to the definition of socioeconomic disadvantage, additional variables were added to the definition of family dysfunction and were linked to the variance in negative treatment outcome explained by family dysfunction. Variables that were added to the definition included negative life stress or high family stress (Kazdin, 1990; Webster-Stratton, 1985, 1990a), cognitive factors of the parents, such as their perceptions of their children's behavior (Dumas & Albin, 1986; Webster-Stratton, 1985, 1990a), marital discord (Dadds, Schwartz, & Sanders, 1987; Dumas, Blechman, & Prinz, 1992; Prinz & Miller, 1994; Webster-Stratton, 1990c), parental substance abuse (Prinz & Miller, 1994), and parental criminal record (Prinz & Miller, 1994). Negative life stress refers to life events such as relocation of a family, a family death, and unemployment that increase the general stress level of the family. To measure the mother's perception of her child's problematic behavior, standardized behavior rating scales were completed by the mother upon intake. Externalizing behavior ratings in the clinical range indicated the mother to perceive her child to have a high level of behavioral distress.

As with the variable, socioeconomic disadvantage, researchers have expanded the definition of the broad-based category of family dysfunction over time. More specific variables have been found that better explain the variance of the association between family dysfunction and negative treatment outcomes during the last 20 years of BPT research. Since the mid 1990s, BPT outcome studies have continued to expand the list of variables subsumed under the category of family dysfunction. New variables listed in the literature as increasing the level of family dysfunction that is adversely related to positive treatment outcomes are poor parental interpersonal relations (Prinz & Miller, 1996), poor parental health (Prinz & Miller, 1996), and adverse and harsh child-rearing practices (Kazdin, Holland, & Crowley, 1997). These variables together with those previously mentioned from earlier years of research form a list of the specific variables predictive of negative treatment outcomes generally referred to as family dysfunction.

Severity of the Child's Conduct Problems

The third characteristic, severity of the child's externalizing behavior, is different from the first two in that it is similarly defined across studies, and is not an umbrella term for a number of smaller variables closely associated. In general, this variable is defined as the intensity and frequency of the child's conduct problems and antisocial behaviors present at the time of treatment. Some minor variation has occurred in the definition of this variable across studies, resulting often from the measures used to define the problem behaviors. However, for the majority of studies, the meaning has referred to the severity of dysfunction of the referred child.

In a study conducted by Kazdin (1990), a number of measures of child dysfunction were assessed and entered into a discriminant function analysis to determine which, if any, aspects of child dysfunction were predictive of negative treatment outcomes. An interview was used to assess the total number of conduct disorder symptoms and antisocial behaviors exhibited by the child, using the Diagnostic and Statistical Manual of Mental Disorders (American Psychiatric Association, 1994). Also included as measures of child dysfunction were the total number of delinquency behaviors based on a self-report measure, and the behavior problem score on the Child Behavior Checklist (CBCL; Achenbach & Edelbrock, 1983). Kazdin found that out of the four measures of child dysfunction utilized, only two, the total number of conduct disorder symptoms and the self-reported delinquency, were predictive of negative treatment outcomes in BPT programs. The results of this study indicated that one of the ways families who experience negative treatment outcomes differ from those who do not was the severity of the dysfunction of the referred child, specifically in the number of Conduct Disorder symptoms and delinquent behaviors reported at the beginning of treatment.

Summary

The BPT literature on contextual variables associated with negative treatment outcomes indicates three consistently mentioned characteristics predictive of poor outcomes: socioeconomic disadvantage, family dysfunction, and severity of the child's externalizing behaviors. The third characteristic, severity of the child's externalizing behavior, is defined as the intensity and frequency of the child's conduct problems and delinquent behaviors presented at the time of treatment (Kazdin, 1990, 1995). This literature affirms the importance of these contextual variables in the treatment of this population, and suggests that these variables may strongly influence the overall effectiveness of BPT for families presenting to treatment with contextual stressors.

Given the neverending goal of psychologists to identify what treatment is best suited for a certain type of person with a particular problem under specific circumstances (Goldfried & Wolfe, 1998; Kazdin & Weisz, 1998; Lonigan et al., 1998), knowledge of negative treatment outcomes in BPT programs and particular circumstances and factors that are predictive of their occurrence is critical. The existing research on negative treatment outcomes reviewed in this article suggests that BPT programs as they currently exist may not be best suited for parents who have a preschool child with disruptive behavior problems and a number of contextual, life stressors. However, it seems premature to stop referring parents with contextual life stressors to BPT programs as a result of this literature because many elements of the relationship between contextual life stressors and negative treatment outcomes are poorly understood at this time.

First, more research is needed to determine which contextual life stressors are critical to the relationship between contextual stressors and negative treatment outcomes. Many variables have been identified as contextual stressors and as such are associated with negative treatment outcomes, but the amount of variance explained by a particular stressor is not clear. It is not yet clear whether the relationship between contextual stressors and negative treatment outcomes is primarily the result of one or two contextual variables or if it is additive, resulting in a stronger relationship the more contextual variables are present. Knowledge of which contextual stressors are critical to the relationship or how many are necessary for the relationship to exist will allow clinicians to make decisions about the probability of a given family entering treatment to experience negative treatment outcomes.

Second, research is needed on the differential effect of contextual stressors on various treatments. Assuming that research can provide knowledge of which contextual stressors or how many stressors are critical to the relationship with negative treatment outcomes, we cannot assume that all BPT programs are the same despite similar basic principles. Research that examines whether families with the same contextual stressors experience similar treatment outcomes despite different BPT programs would provide valuable information about the role of contextual stressors, the BPT curriculum, or subtle treatment process differences in this relationship. In addition, families with the same contextual stressors who enter treatment other than BPT could be added to the comparison to determine whether the basic principles underlying BPT play an important role in the relationship or whether the more central variables are the contextual stressors themselves.

Third, research is needed to determine how contextual life stressors impact the treatment process. Before we can identify what type of treatment is best suited for families with multiple contextual stressors and a child with conduct problems, we must understand the relationship between contextual stressors and the treatment process. Specifically, we must understand how the identified contextual variables impact and influence the treatment process, and identify the underlying mechanisms of the relationship between the contextual stressors and negative treatment outcomes. To obtain this information, it seems critical that the perspective of the treatment participants experiencing the contextual stressors as they impact treatment, and experiencing the treatment process as it impacts their life condition be solicited and analyzed. Qualitative research provides an optimal methodology for empirically obtaining the perspective of the parents. Through qualitative research, the parents' perspectives can be gathered, interpreted, and reported as a theoretical formulation of their experience (Strauss & Corbin, 1990). To date, no qualitative studies have examined the perceptions of parents with multiple pretreatment risk factors as to how contextual and treatment process variables influence BPT for their family.

Finally, once it is determined which contextual life stressors are critical to understanding the relationship between contextual stressors and negative treatment outcomes, what the differential effect of contextual stressors have on various treatments, and how contextual life stressors impact the treatment process, research will have to identify treatment that could effect the mechanisms underlying the relationship between contextual stressors and treatment outcomes. This new treatment or changes to the treatment process will diffuse the existing relationship between contextual stressors and negative treatment outcomes, and allow families with such stressors to experience the many short and long-term benefits typically associated with behavioral parent training programs.

REFERENCES

Achenbach, T. M., & Edelbrock, C. S. (1983). Manual for the child behavior checklist and revised child behavior profile. Burlington, VT: University Associates in Psychiatry.

American Psychiatric Association. (1994). Diagnostic and statistical manual of mental disorders (4th ed.). Washington, DC: Author.

Armbruster, P., & Fallon, T. (1994). Clinical, sociodemographic, and systems risk factors for attrition in a children's mental health clinic. American Journal of Orthopsychiatry, 64, 577–585.

Bernal, M. E. (1984). Consumer issues in parent training. In R. F. Dangel & R. A. Polster (Eds.), Parent training: Foundations of research and practice. New York: Guilford Press.

Bernal, M. E., Klinnert, M. D., & Schultz, L. A. (1980). Outcome evaluation of behavioral parent training and client-centered parent counseling for children with conduct problems. Journal of Applied Behavior Analysis, 13, 677–691.

Brestan, E. V., & Eyberg, S. M. (1998). Effective psychosocial treatments of conduct-disordered children and adolescents: 29 years, 82 studies, and 5,272 kids. Journal of Clinical Child Psychology, 27, 180–189.

Brestan, E. V., Eyberg, S. M., Boggs, S., & Algina, J. (1997). Parent-child interaction therapy: Parent perceptions of untreated siblings. Child and Family Behavior Therapy, 19, 13–28.

Campbell, S. B. (1994). Hard-to-manage preschool boys: Externalizing behavior, social competence, and family context at two-year followup. Journal of Abnormal Child Psychology, 22, 147–166.

Cataldo, M. F. (1984). Clinical considerations in training parents of children with special problems. In R. F. Dangel, & R. A. Polster (Eds.), Parent training: Foundations of research and practice (pp. 329–503). New York: Guilford Press.

Chamberlain, P., & Baldwin, D. V. (1987). Client resistance to parent training: Its therapeutic management. In T. R. Kratochwill (Ed.), Advances in school psychology (Vol. 6.) New York: Plenum.

Dadds, M. R., Schwartz, S., & Sanders, M. R. (1987). Marital discord and treatment outcome in behavioral treatment of child conduct disorders. Journal of Consulting and Clinical Psychology, 55, 396–403.

Dumas, J. E. (1984). Child, adult-interactional, and socioeconomic setting events as predictors of parent training outcome. Education and Treatment of Children, 7, 351–364.

Dumas, J. E., & Albin, J. B. (1986). Parent training outcome: Does active parental involvement matter? Behavior Research and Therapy, 24, 227–230.

Dumas, J. E., Blechman, E. A., & Prinz, R. J. (1992). Helping families with aggressive children and adolescents change. In R. D. Peters & R. J. McMahon (Eds.), Aggression and violence throughout the life span (pp. 126–154). Thousand Oaks, CA: Sage Publications.

Dumas, J. E., & Wahler, R. G. (1983). Predictors of treatment outcome in parent training: Mother insularity and socioeconomic disadvantage. Behavioral Assessment, 5, 301–313.

Eisenstadt, T. H., Eyberg, S. M., McNeil, C. B., Newcomb, K., & Funderburk, B. (1993). Parent-child interaction therapy with behavior problem children: Relative effectiveness of two stages and overall treatment outcome. Journal of Clinical Child Psychology, 22, 42–51.

Eyberg, S., & Boggs, S. R. (1998). Parent-child interaction therapy: A psychosocial intervention for the treatment of young conduct-disordered children. In J. M. Briesmeister, & C. E. Schaefer (Eds.), Handbook of parent training: Parents as co-therapists for children's behavior problems (2nd ed., pp. 61–97). New York: Wiley.

Eyberg, S., Boggs, S. R., & Rodriguez, C. M. (1992). Relationships between maternal parenting stress and child disruptive behavior. Child and Family Behavior Therapy, 14, 1–10.

Eyberg, S. M., & Johnson, S. M. (1974). Multiple assessment of behavior modification with families: Effects of contingency contracting and order of treated families. Journal of Consulting and Clinical Psychology, 42, 594–606.

Eyberg, S. M., & Robinson, E. A. (1982). Parent-child interaction training: Effects on family functioning. Journal of Clinical Child Psychology, 11, 130–137.

Forehand, R. L., Breiner, J., McMahon, R. J., & Davies, G. (1981). Predictors of cross setting behavior change in the treatment of child problems. Journal of Behavior Therapy and Experimental Psychiatry, 12, 311–313.

Forehand, R. L., Furey, W. M., & McMahon, R. J. (1984). The role of maternal distress in parent training to modify child noncompliance. Behavioral Psychotherapy, 12, 93–108.

Forehand, R., & Kotchick, B. A. (1996). Cultural diversity: A wake-up call for parent training. Behavior Therapy, 27, 187–206.

Forehand, R., & Long, N. (1988). Outpatient treatment of the acting out child: Procedures, long term follow-up data, and clinical problems. Advances in Behavior Research and Therapy, 10, 117–129.

Forehand, R. L., & McMahon, R. J. (1981). Helping the noncompliant child: A clinician's guide to parent training. New York: Guilford Press.

Forehand, R., Middlebrook, J., Rogers, T., & Steffe, M. (1983). Dropping out of parent training. Behavior Research and Therapy, 21, 663–668.

Forehand, R., Rogers, T., Steffe, M., & Middlebrook, J. (1984). Helping parents help their noncompliant child. Journal of Child and Adolescent Psychotherapy, 1, 6–10.

Goldfried, M. R., & Wolfe, B. E. (1998). Toward a more clinically valid approach to therapy research. Journal of Consulting and Clinical Psychology, 66, 143–150.

Gould, M. S., Shaffer, D., & Kaplan, D. (1985). The characteristics of dropouts from a child psychiatric clinic. Journal of the American Academy of Child Psychiatry, 24, 316–328.

Griest, D. L., Forehand, R., & Wells, K. C. (1981). Follow-up assessment of parent behavioral training: An analysis of who will participate. Child Study Journal, 11, 221–229.

Henry, S. A. (1985). An experimental analysis of the Forehand-McMahon compliance training program for the treatment of noncompliance in preschoolers. Dissertation Abstracts International, 45 (8-B), 2689.

Jacobsen, N. S., Follette, W. C., & Revenstorf, D. (1984). Psychotherapy outcome research: Methods for reporting variability and evaluating clinical significance. Behavior Therapy, 15, 336–352.

Jahn, D. L., & Lichstein, K. L. (1980). The resistive client: A neglected phenomenon in behavior therapy. Behavior Modification, 4, 303–320.

Kazdin, A. E. (1987). Conduct disorders in childhood and adolescence. Newbury Park, CA: Sage.

Kazdin, A. E. (1990). Premature termination from treatment among children referred for antisocial behavior. Journal of Child Psychology and Psychiatry and Allied Disciplines, 31, 415–425.

Kazdin, A. E. (1995). Conduct disorders in childhood and adolescence. (2nd ed.), Thousand Oaks, CA: Sage.

Kazdin, A. E. (1997). Parent management training: Evidence, outcomes, and issues. Journal of the American Academy of Child and Adolescent Psychiatry, 36, 1349–1356.

Kazdin, A. E., Holland, L., & Crowley, M. (1997). Family experience of barriers to treatment and premature termination from child therapy. Journal of Consulting and Clinical Psychology, 65, 453–463.

Kazdin, A. E., Holland, L., Crowley, M., & Breton, S. (1997). Barriers to treatment participation scale: Evaluation and validation in the context of child outpatient treatment. Journal of Child Psychology and Psychiatry, 38, 1051–1062.

Kazdin, A. E., Mazurick, J. L., & Siegel, T. C. (1994). Treatment outcome among children with externalizing disorder who terminate prematurely versus those who complete psychotherapy. Journal of the American Academy of Child and Adolescent Psychiatry, 33, 549–557.

Kazdin, A. E., & Wassell, G. (1999). Barriers to treatment participation and therapeutic change among children referred for conduct disorder. Journal of Clinical Child Psychology, 28, 160–172.

Kazdin, A. E., & Weisz, J. R. (1998). Identifying and developing empirically supported child and adolescent treatments. Journal of Consulting and Clinical Psychology, 66, 19–36.

Long, P., Forehand, R., Wierson, M., & Morgan, A. (1994). Does parent training with young noncompliant children have long-term effects? Advances in Behavior Research and Therapy, 32, 101–107.

Lonigan, C. J., Elbert, J. C., & Johnson, S. B. (1998). Empirically supported psychosocial interventions for children: An overview. Journal of Clinical Child Psychology, 27, 138–145.

McMahon, R. J., & Forehand, R. (1984). Parent training for the noncompliant child: Treatment outcome, generalization, and adjunctive therapy procedures. In R. F. Dangel & R. A. Polster (Eds.), Parent training: Foundations of research and practice (pp. 298–328). New York: Guilford.

McMahon, R. J., Forehand, R., & Griest, D. L. (1981). Effects of knowledge of social learning principles on enhancing treatment outcome and generalization in a parent training program. Journal of Consulting and Clinical Psychology, 49, 526–532.

McMahon, R. J., & Wells, K. C. (1998). Conduct problems. In E. J. Mash & R. A. Barkley (Eds.), Treatment of childhood disorders (pp. 111–207). New York: Guilford Press.

McNeil, C. B., Eyberg, S. M., Eisenstadt, T. H., Newcomb, K., & Funderburk, B. W. (1991). Parent–child interaction therapy with behavior problem children: Generalization of treatment effects to the school setting. Journal of Clinical Child Psychology, 20, 140–151.

Miller, G. E., & Prinz, R. J. (1990). Enhancement of social learning family interventions for childhood conduct disorder. Psychological Bulletin, 108(2), 291–307.

Patterson, G. R., Reid, J. B, Jones, R. R., & Conger, R. E. (1975). A social learning approach to family intervention: Families with aggressive children (Vol. 1). Eugene, OR: Castalia.

Peed, S., Roberts, M., & Forehand, R. (1977). Evaluation of the effectiveness of a standardized parent training program in altering the interaction of mothers and their noncompliant children. Behavior Modification, 1, 323–350.

Prinz, R. J., & Miller, G. E. (1994). Family-based treatment for childhood antisocial behavior: Experimental influences on dropout and engagement. Journal of Consulting and Clinical Psychology, 62, 645–650.

Prinz, R. J., & Miller, G. E. (1996). Parental engagement in interventions for children at risk for conduct disorder. In R. D. Peters and R. J. McMahon (Eds.), Preventing childhood disorders, substance abuse, and delinquency (pp.161–183). Thousand Oaks, CA: Sage Publications.

Serketich, W. J., & Dumas, J. E. (1996). The effectiveness of behavioral parent training to modify antisocial behavior in children: A meta-analysis. Behavior Therapy, 27, 171–186.

Stoiber, K. C., & Kratochwill, T. R. (2000). Empirically supported interventions and school psychology: Rationale and methodological issues—Part I. School Psychology Quarterly, 15, 75–105.

Strauss, A., & Corbin, J. (1990). Basics of qualitative research: Grounded theory procedures and techniques. Thousand Oaks, CA: Sage Publications.

Tremblay, R. E., Pagani-Kurtz, L., Masse, L. C., Vitaro, F., & Phil, R. (1995). A bimodal preventive intervention for disruptive kindergarten boys: Its impact through mid-adolescence. Journal of Consulting and Clinical Psychology, 63, 560–568.

Tremblay, R. E., Vitaro, F., Bertrand, L., LeBlanc, M., Beauchesne, H., Boileau, H., & Lucille, D. (1992). Parent and child training to prevent early onset of delinquency: The Montreal longitudinal experimental study. In J. McCord & R. E. Tremblay (Eds.), Preventing antisocial behavior: Interventions from birth through adolescence (pp. 117–138). New York: Guilford Press.

Wahler, R. G. (1980). The insular mother: Her problems in parent-child treatment. Journal of Applied Behavior Analysis, 13, 207–219.

Wahler, R. G., Leske, G., & Rogers, E. S. (1979). The insular family: A deviance support system for oppositional children. In L. A. Hamerlynck (Ed.), Behavioral systems for the developmentally disabled: Vol. 1. School and family environments (pp. 102–127). New York: Brunner/Mazel.

Webster-Stratton, C. (1981a). Teaching mothers through videotape modeling to change their children's behavior. Behavior Therapy, 12, 634–642.

Webster-Stratton, C. (1981b). Videotape modeling: A method of parenting education. Journal of Clinical Child Psychology, 10, 93–97.

Webster-Stratton, C. (1982). The long-term effects of a videotape modeling parent-training program: Comparison of immediate and 1-year follow-up results. Behavior Therapy, 13, 702–714.

Webster-Stratton, C. (1984). Randomized trial of two parent-training programs for families with conduct-disordered children. Journal of Consulting and Clinical Psychology, 52, 666–678.

Webster-Stratton, C. (1985). Predictors of treatment outcome in parent training for conduct disordered children. Behavior Therapy, 16, 223–243.

Webster-Stratton, C. (1990a). Enhancing the effectiveness of self-administered videotape parent training for families with conduct-problem children. Journal of Abnormal Child Psychology, 18, 479–492.

Webster-Stratton, C. (1990b). Long-term follow-up of families with young conduct problem children: From preschool to grade school. Journal of Consulting and Clinical Psychology, 19, 144–149.

Webster-Stratton, C. (1990c). Predictors of treatment outcome in parent training for families with conduct problem children. Behavior Therapy, 21, 319–337.

Webster-Stratton, C. (1993). Strategies for helping early school-aged children with oppositional defiant disorders and/or conduct disorders: The importance of home-school connections. School Psychology Review, 22, 437–457.

Webster-Stratton, C. (1994). Advancing videotape parent training: A comparison study. Journal of Consulting and Clinical Psychology, 62, 583–593.

Webster-Stratton, C. (1998). Preventing conduct problems in Head Start children: Strengthening parent competencies. Journal of Consulting and Clinical Psychology, 66, 715–730.

Webster-Stratton, C., & Hammond, M. (1997). Treating children with early-onset conduct problems: A comparison of child and parent training interventions. Journal of Consulting and Clinical Psychology, 65, 93–109.

Wiltz, N. A., & Patterson, G. R. (1974). An evaluation of parent training procedures designed to alter inappropriate aggressive behavior of boys. Behavior Therapy, 5, 215–221.